A LONDON MERCHANT
1695–1774

A
LONDON MERCHANT
1695–1774

By

LUCY S. SUTHERLAND

FRANK CASS & COMPANY LTD

OXFORD UNIVERSITY PRESS

1962

First published by Oxford University Press in 1933

FIRST EDITION 1933
REPRINTED 1962

Published by Frank Cass & Company Ltd.,
10 *Woburn Walk, London, W.C.*1

Printed in Great Britain by
Taylor Garnett Evans & Co. Ltd.,
Watford and London

PREFACE

WHEN Malachy Postlethwayt suggested that a Mercantile College should preserve, as examples of the greatness of their craft, the 'accounts of many distinguished and eminent merchants deceased...who trod the Royal Exchange with supreme credit and dignity'[1] he spoke in the height of commercial pride which was reached in the eighteenth century, before the challenge of industry and an economic interpretation based on its predominance brought its sobering influence to bear on 'the great mercantile classes of England'. In a wider sense, now that that age with all its vigorous yet obscurely developed commercialism has become perhaps more difficult to estimate than its predecessors in commerce as well as in politics, because its similarities to succeeding ages serve to mask its differences, we can echo his wish for the books of a Sir Theodore Janssen, a Sir Peter Delmé, or a Sir Henry Furnese.

In default of the books of these merchant princes which would show not only the extent of their traffic but its adaptation to the trend of their time, interest attaches to any consecutive collection of accounts of prominent merchants which chance may have saved from destruction. Worthy illustrations of this type of records, unfortunately so scarce, are the papers of William Braund, merchant, shipowner, and shipping insurer, Director of the East India Company and of the Sun Fire Office. The papers, which consist almost wholly of accounts, cover, with a few gaps, and not with equal thoroughness, the years 1741–74, when he died in prosperous commercial ease at the age of seventy-eight.

These papers are in the possession of Champion Russell, Esq., of Stubbers, Essex, to whom I am indebted for their use, as also for much kindness and help in local and family history. They came to Stubbers about 1774, after the death of their owner, as John Russell, Esq., the husband of Braund's niece, was one of the three executors appointed under his

---

[1] M. Postlethwayt, *Universal Dictionary of Commerce*. (The first edition of this work appeared in 1751–5. That quoted here throughout is the fourth and fullest edition of 1774.)

will. They consist of a number of volumes bound in calf, canvas and cardboard, and some loose papers. They include, besides two ledgers of William Braund and various of his journals and cash-books, the shipping papers of his brother and business associate, Samuel Braund, who predeceased him. The latter cover the years 1747 to 1760, when Samuel retired from business.

A study of William Braund himself would be of little interest; there is nothing in him or his life that raises him above his type. A study of certain aspects of commercial life in the eighteenth century through the medium of his activities seems, on the other hand, both interesting and valuable. It is this I have undertaken. This study is thus presented to the reader as an essay in what the Americans had called, rather infelicitously, 'business history', in the economic mechanism of a certain state of society.

I am deeply indebted to R. T. Berthon, Esq., of Salsey, Chichester, for help in all questions of genealogy and for placing at my disposal a manuscript embodying the results of long research into family history. I am also under a heavy obligation to Warren Dawson, Esq., Honorary Librarian of Lloyd's, for help in my chapter on Marine Insurance, and to Professor Namier for reading the whole and giving me his valuable advice. To Professor G. N. Clark I am very much indebted for help and advice in the correction of the proofs. My thanks are also due to Miss M. V. Clarke, of Somerville College, for much advice and assistance. I wish to thank the Editor of the *Economic History Review* for permission to reprint here as Chapter II the greater part of an article published in his pages. Somerville College has generously made a grant in aid of the publication of this book.

L. S. S.

1933

CONTENTS

CONTENTS

I

WILLIAM BRAUND, MERCHANT, 1695-1774

WILLIAM BRAUND, the subject of this study, has nothing to distinguish him from any one of the thousands of merchants who throve in eighteenth-century London. Hacton, his solid, well-built, mid-Georgian house in Essex, with its fine staircase, its square rooms of a size domestic rather than spacious, its heavy doors with their double bolts, its park and its well-stocked kitchen garden, gives an impression of sober prosperity and good husbandry. It is the property of a man who has done well, who knows and likes the pleasant life of the English country house, but who, when he comes to live it himself, has no intention of wasting his hard-earned wealth in profusion of living. Beyond this quality of commercial solidity he has left witness of few outstanding characteristics. A man may often be known by his books, but what remain of the brown calf volumes that once filled the shelves of his library are so much what might be expected that they give no indication of his character. In the fine eighteenth-century library at Stubbers are to be found some of these books, which were scattered among his many nephews on the death of the favourite one, who was his heir; Tindal's *Christianity as old as the Creation : or the Gospel a Republication of the Religion of Nature* (1730); Dugdale's *Monasticon* (the second English abridgement of 1718, bought for £1 6s. 6d.); Locke's *Works* (the three volume edition of 1722), as well as those, rather surprisingly, of James I. For lighter reading there were Ben Jonson's *Comedies* and the second edition of Gay's *Beggar's Opera*.[1] In connexion with his business there is Beawes' *Lex Mercatoria Rediviva* (1752), for which he was a subscriber, and William Bolts' *State of Bengal* (1772), carefully marked in a way which indicates his side in the party disputes of the East India Company. Then, finally, in his last years when, an old man, he retired

---

[1] The Devonshire Braunds were connected by marriage with the Gays, so that it is possible, as Mr. R. T. Berthon suggests, that William Braund may have bought the book on account of this connexion with the family.

to the life of a country gentleman, there are the works of Arthur Young, then at the height of their popularity; *The Farmer's Letters* (1767), *The Northern Tour* (1770), and *Rural Œconomy : or Essays on the practical parts of Husbandry* (1770). They are a sober collection, less personal even than those of his still dimmer brother Samuel which may be found with them; for Samuel side by side with Carkesse's *Rates of Merchandise* bought Pope as he came out, liked translations from the French, the religion of nature, and the semi-scientific publications of that age, such as Ray's *Wisdom of God Manifested in the Works of the Creation*, and Leybourn's geometrical and astronomical problems, *Pleasure with Profit*. In religion William was a member of the Established Church ; in politics he passed the 1745 test of Whiggism, for he signed the declaration of the London merchants that they would accept Bank Bills during the crisis caused by the Jacobite rising. His business associates, Brice Fisher and Linwood, were in touch with the Newcastle administration, but he had no such connexion. The only broadsheet found among his papers, *To the Worthy Liverymen of the Free City of London* [1754], appeals on the contrary to that Whiggish anti-ministerialism so common among the mass of City merchants.

The Braunds were of North Devon yeoman stock, settled at Black Torrington since at least the sixteenth century and probably much earlier. William's father, Benjamin Braund, citizen and vintner of London, when he came up to London for his apprenticeship was the first of his family to leave Devon. He prospered in the capital, and as owner for many years of the Rummer Tavern in Queen Street was believed to have 'acquired a plentiful fortune'.[1] He died in 1734. William was the second of his three sons. That Benjamin was, or had been, well-to-do is suggested not only by the fact that he retired in his old age to a house in Essex at Corbets-Tey, Upminster, but by the provision he made for his family. He had set up his eldest son, Benjamin, in the lucrative but expensive calling of commander of an East Indiaman, paid a consideration of

---

[1] *Daily Journal*, Saturday, 13 July 1734. Brit. Mus. Burney Collection of early newspapers, vol. 304 B.

£300 for the apprenticeship of his second son, William, and £200 for that of his youngest son, Samuel, and endowed and married his two daughters, the one Mary, 'the Belle of Essex', to Champion Branfill, Esq., of Upminster Hall, Essex, the other less ambitiously to Leonard Pead, Clothworker and Common Council-man for Cheap Ward, London.

In his later years, however, misfortune seems to have fallen on him, for he laments in his will the fact that, through circumstances of which they are all aware, he can now leave little to his family. To his two younger sons, William and Samuel, whom he had not, he says, 'fully advanced' (though both being over thirty-five, they must already have been engaged in their callings), he left all his real estate, consisting of two freehold properties in London, in Crane Court, off Fleet Street, and in Bucklersbury.[1] Samuel, of whom very little can be discovered, for even his will cannot be traced, seems never to have been a merchant proper. Though apprenticed in 1714 to William Billers, Citizen and Haberdasher,[2] he had possibly always acted as one of those intermediaries who were springing up like mushrooms to meet the growing needs of London commerce. In the years from 1748 to 1760, when he and William had a good deal of business in common, he was one of a very important type of intermediary, a 'ship's husband' in the supply of shipping for the East India Company. In 1760, already of good years, he retired suddenly from business, probably through ill-health, and six years later died. William, on the other hand, was apprenticed in 1712 to a merchant, Christopher Emmett of London,[3] and remained during the greater part of his life a merchant, a Portugal merchant in the first half of the century when the commercial policy

[1] William would seem to have transferred his half share to his brother after 1743, for the references disappear from his accounts, but they reappear on his brother's death in 1766. The Crane Court property consisted of two houses, valued in 1773 at £1,600. They brought in a rent of only £15 a year, as Samuel Braund lived in one of them. The Bucklersbury property consisted of one house, valued at £1,000 in 1773, which brought in a rent of £65–70.

[2] *Apprenticeship records.* Record Office copy at Society of Genealogists. I.N.L. 1/8, fo. 89. From MS. *ut sup.* in possession of R. T. Berthon, Esq.

[3] I.N.I. 1/1, fo. 105, ibid. *The London Magazine*, 1746, p. 154, announcing the death of Christopher Emmett, Esq., called him 'One of the most eminent Merchants of this City'.

of the Methuen Treaty was in force and trade flourished greatly between Portugal and England. The first merchant directory for London in the eighteenth century is not found till 1738, four years after his father's death. He is there described as a merchant of Rood Lane, Fenchurch Street. The directory of 1744 gives to him and his brother Samuel the address of Tokenhouse Yard. By 1757 he had moved to Copthall Court, Throgmorton Street; by 1763 either to Coleman Street or Broad Street, for the two directories of that year give him different addresses. In 1766 his address was Russia Court, Leadenhall Street, where he was joined by his favourite nephew, Benjamin Branfill, just returned from Lisbon. In 1768 he made his last move, with Branfill, to Fenchurch Street, but he was an old man by then, and his use of his office became increasingly nominal.[1] In 1774 he died at the good age of seventy-eight, worth on his own estimate £45,000, and was buried in his vault outside Upminster Church, Essex.

The life of such a man, and still more his interest to any one examining his life, depends much on his milieu and connexions. Family, locality, and the relationships established in trade make up the environment which determines almost entirely the course of his existence. To the average merchant living the life of an individualist but with a spirit of the most cautious conservatism, they are at once his refuge and his responsibility in a complex competitive world. Braund's life was mostly passed in the City, on 'Change, in Lloyd's Coffee-house, or his City offices. In all he had the small safe shelter of his ' connexions', sound men whom he had known personally for years, between whom and himself there was mutual trust, and who changed only with retirement from business or with death. Behind them, and, indeed, mixed up considerably with them (for he had relatives in trade, and his business connexions married into his family), were his family, and behind them again lay a certain part of Essex, the flat lands of the lower reaches of the Thames, Upminster, Romford, Chigwell, and Hornchurch, which was the concrete expression of the solidarity and permanence which he knew. It was here that his father died,

---

[1] London Directories in the British Museum and Guildhall Libraries.

that his brother Benjamin had his house till he died in India in 1738, that his sister Mary was married, bore in twelve years her twelve children, was widowed and died, that his sister Ann Pead came to live when she became a widow. It was here that he lived when he was out of town himself, at first (for he was a bachelor) with his widowed sister Mary Branfill, to whose children he acted almost as a father, and whose marriages, most of them in the neighbourhood, he approved and arranged. And here he finally built his own house, retired, and died.

The spread of Londoners over the surrounding counties was in the eighteenth century very spectacular. Attention was drawn not only to the great merchant who, having made his fortune, sought to expunge the taint of trade by the correctness of his life as a country gentleman, but also to lesser men, the 'cit' who made himself a small estate within reach of the City, where his family could spend the summer, where he could go for the week-ends, and to which he could eventually retire. This movement comprised not only that of the Londoner to the country but the return to the country of those whom the capital had drawn into it. In the churches of the Home Counties inscriptions and lists of benefactions bear witness to the numbers of worthy tradesmen and merchants of London who returned to die in the villages where they had been born. The movement was not, of course, new, and Essex, although less touched by the double exodus in the eighteenth century than Middlesex, Surrey, or Berkshire, had already been deeply penetrated by merchants. Within an easy day's ride of London, and the easiest way out of the seafaring part of the City, Stepney, Poplar, and Ratcliffe Cross, it was inevitable that it should appeal to the retired merchant, and still more to the retired sea-captain, or to others who had, in the eighteenth-century phrase, 'provided for themselves in the seafaring way'. In the district with which Braund was connected, as early as the fourteenth century the manor of Warley-Franks was owned by a citizen of London.[1] The three families with whom he was connected by marriage, the Russells of Stubbers, the

[1] P. Morant, *The History and Antiquities of the County of Essex*, 1768, i. 112.

Branfills of Upminster Hall, and the Harrisons of Hornchurch, and then of Chigwell Row come within this class.
Stubbers was acquired about 1689 by Sir William Russell,
citizen and Alderman of London. The Manor of Upminster was bought in 1685 from the Earl of Gainsborough
by Captain Andrew Branfill of Ratcliffe. The Harrisons
were a family connected with the affairs of the East India
Company. In the eighteenth century the Braund family
established themselves in the same way, and, later, William's
neighbour, Sir James Esdaile the banker, bought the
Manor of Gaines. It was, in short, a district where the
connexion between wealth and commerce was still recent,
and where, in a way that had ceased to be common at that
time among the established gentry, the younger son could
still naturally seek his fortune in commerce in the City.
Yet whatever may be the general truth of Mr. Tawney's[1]
contention that it was the turning of the merchant to the
land which as much as anything furthered the commer-
cialization of English agriculture, the commercial society
of this part of Essex had done nothing of the kind. Their
wealth was made elsewhere, and the land was only a safe
investment for an old age of ease, and for their heirs who
need no longer take part in the struggle for existence.
They were no improving landlords. Though the London
market was near at hand, this was a conservative, backward
district, where in some places the open field system lingered
till the end of the eighteenth century. Though there was,
of course, as throughout Essex, a good deal of enclosed
land, it took the form for the most part of small farms or
moderate sized parks, and the common rights were on the
whole well sustained.

William Braund is a good example of the merchant who,
during his active life, kept some connexion with the country, and when he retired from business settled down there
to pass his old age in peace and dignity. Through many
years he lived, in the short intervals when out of Town,
with his widowed sister Mary Branfill at Upminster Hall.
Local tradition has it that he finally quarrelled with her on

[1] R. H. Tawney, *The Agrarian Problem in the Sixteenth Century*, 1912, pp.
187–8, 351, 383.

the subject of a black servant, and that he then left her house, bought the land of Hacton from her, and built his own.[1] There may be truth in the tradition, but there is not in his accounts any evidence of a serious breach with his sister, and his name remained in her will as her executor; moreover, though he bought the farm of Hacton earlier,[2] he did not begin to enlarge the estate or to build until two years after her death. When he began to build Hacton, it was a long and serious matter, for the house took four years to complete, and the cost of the whole estate was calculated at £4,000. He made his own bricks, and contracted with a builder called Babb, to whom he paid instalments of the price almost monthly. So far as the accounts show, the builder was also the architect, for the only entry which bears on the question of planning is 'paid J. Burnell for plans £5 5s.' The contract with the builder must have covered the mere shell of the house, for the plumber, the mason, the painters, and the carpenters were paid separately by Braund himself, as their work was required. The carpenters seem to have made most of the furniture locally, though there is a special payment for chairs, and the carpet was bought from John Fisher,[3] a London business connexion, and long ells for an undefined purpose were supplied by Thomas Burfoot, his packer in London employed in his Portuguese trade. When it was finished he continued to enlarge its grounds, to build a mill and a barn (the latter at a price of £333 11s.), until on his death the estimated value of the estate was £7,539.[4] Here in the last three years of his life he lived entirely, managing his estate and buying and selling stock.[5] A few

[1] *The Essex Naturalist*, 1888–9.
[2] The incompleteness of the early accounts prevents the discovery when he bought his two estates at Upminster, Hunts and Hacton. He possessed neither in 1743, but in 1758, when his ledgers begin, he owned the farm of Hunts and the small farm of Hacton, the nucleus of his later estate, yielding a rent of only £12 4s. a year.
[3] Partner and relative of Brice Fisher, see *infra*, p. 13, n. 2.
[4] When Braund decided to build he bought two pieces of land adjacent to the farm of Hacton for £1,000. The additions he made to his estate, consisted of the leasing in 1767 of two pieces of land, Brookhill Grove and Hogland Spring for £43 a year, the purchase in 1768 of a farm to add to it for £1,000, and in 1771 the acquisition of four more fields of about 28 acres from Sir James Esdaile, partly by exchange, partly by purchase, for £95 7s. 10d.
[5] His other investments in land were all within reach of Upminster in the Essex

signs of his old occupation remain; his books are kept to the month of his death with meticulous commercial care, and he began to sell the bricks made on his estate. In other ways his interests became entirely those of a country gentleman. A typical land dispute is that between him and his neighbour Sir James Esdaile of the manor of Gaines. They had fallen out over a misunderstanding of the terms of a sale and exchange of lands in 1771.[1] Braund claimed £6 14s. 6d. which Esdaile maintained was unreasonable, and their relations became increasingly bad. Then Esdaile sent his steward to demand that Braund should take down certain posts he had put up in front of his house on the waste of the manor of Gaines. Braund replied with dignity that he had put them up for the convenience of those ' on a Dark Night or in Liquor ', as his friends had suggested that he might be blamed if any one fell into the ditch. If Esdaile insisted, he would remove them, but he felt bound to point out several infringements by Sir James on the rights of the inhabitants, such as taking away their watering places, and building cottages without 4 acres of land, contrary to 31 Elizabeth, c. 7. As Esdaile still refused to pay his demands, and insisted on the removal of the posts, Braund went somewhat further. He obtained several legal opinions on Nuisances and their Redress. Then on 6 August he went to water his horses on the common, found a padlocked gate, and broke the padlock. The next day finding it replaced, he did the same

marshlands. In 1759 he bought the property of Gubions or Gobions in East Tilling from his sister Mary Branfill for £5,000 (£1,200 of which went to the marriage portion of her daughter Amelia). It brought in a rent of about £156 17s. a year, and was valued in 1773 at £6,500. In 1766 he bought three fields of about 9 acres in Hornchurch from John Harrison, husband to his niece, for which he paid £364 and which were valued in 1773 at £438 19s. 4d. In 1769 he bought 11 acres of marshland at Rainham for £420, valued in 1773 at £438 19s. 4d. In 1770 he bought more land, at Mucking, for £574 2s. on which he erected some building at a cost of £237 7s. and from which he drew a rent of £26 16s. It was valued in 1773 at £800. Finally in 1772 he bought of William Wildman, grazier, 18 acres of marshland at Barking, called Whiting's level, for £1,400, Wildman continuing to occupy it at a rent of £49 19s. Wildman appears to have acted as agent for Braund on his own estate.

[1] Braund sold him his farm of Hunts, yielding a rent of £67 4s. a year, for £3,122 13s. 6d. The transaction was complicated by the fact that Braund bought four fields (see p. 7, note 4) from him at the same time.

and also made his wagon knock down the palings. The end of the quarrel, however, does not appear, perhaps it was only stopped by Braund's last illness and death at the beginning of the next year.

The three tables on pp. 10–12 illustrate in a simplified form the Braund family and its connexions. They are so arranged as to bring out particularly the relations of family and business in the connexions of William Braund.

In these tables we see relatives like Leonard Pead and Benjamin Branfill working in close association with Samuel and William Braund. Benjamin Branfill, indeed, the second son of his sister, was the special protégé of William, who put him into the Portugal trade, advancing him considerable sums, and obtaining a partnership for him when a young man of twenty-two in the firm of his English correspondents in Lisbon. When he returned to England about 1767 to manage the English side of the business, Braund and he lived at the same London address. He rose rapidly in the commercial world, becoming in 1771 a Director of the Bank of England, and when Braund died he was left heir to Hacton and almost the whole property. Business associates like Charles Harris and John Harrison, and business acquaintances like Robert James,[1] secretary to the East India Company, and brother-in law of Charles Harris, married into the family. We can also trace the growth, through connexion and the influence growing out of it, of a typical East India family. Within the wide ramifications of the East India Company, the greatest commercial organization of its time, and also a great political administration, the younger members of the families of Braund, Branfill, Cotton, and Harrison sought their fortunes, some in its commercial shipping, some in its army or civil branch, but all equally through the influence, no doubt, of their relatives. It is an illustration of the enormous range of East India Company patronage, a rival in some ways, till the

[1] Robert James was Secretary to the East India Company from 1748 to 1768, a capable official and an honest man who ' had not followed his Predecessors in exacting Perquisities but on the contrary had discouraged them to his own great Loss'. (India Office; East India Company Court Book 69, f. 362, 15 Mar. 1761). He has a high place among the disinterested officials who made the tradition of the home service of the East India Company.

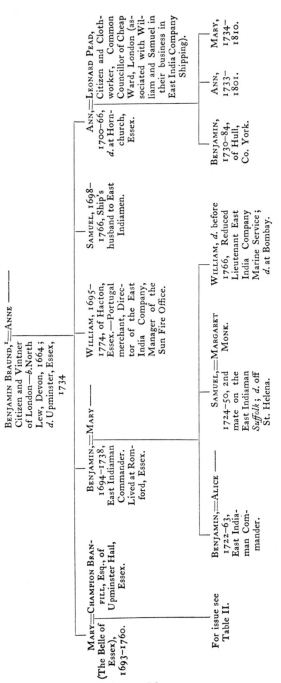

BENJAMIN BRAUND,[1]—ANNE
Citizen and Vintner
of London—b.North
Lew, Devon, 1664;
d. Upminster, Essex,
1734

MARY—CHAMPION BRAN-
(The Belle of FILL, Esq, of
Essex), Upminster Hall,
1693–1760. Essex.

BENJAMIN,—MARY
1694–1738,
East Indiaman
Commander.
Lived at Rom-
ford, Essex.

WILLIAM, 1695–
1774, of Hacton,
Essex.—Portugal
merchant, Direc-
tor of the East
India Company,
Manager of the
Sun Fire Office.

SAMUEL, 1668–
1766, Ship's
husband to East
Indiamen.

ANN,—LEONARD PEAD,
1700–66, Citizen and Cloth-
d. at Horn- worker, Common
church, Councillor of Cheap
Essex. Ward, London (as-
sociated with Wil-
liam and Samuel in
their business in
East India Company
Shipping).

For issue see
Table II.

BENJAMIN,—ALICE
1722–63,
East India-
man Com-
mander.

SAMUEL,—MARGARET
1724–50, 2nd MONK.
mate on the
East Indiaman
Suffolk; d. off
St. Helena.

WILLIAM, d. before
1766, Reduced
Lieutenant East
India Company
Marine Service;
d. at Bombay.

BENJAMIN,
1730–84,
of Hull,
Co. York.

ANN,
1733–
1801.

MARY,
1734–
1810.

10

[1] These tables are simplified for the purpose of bringing out three points : (1) William Braund's connexions in Essex ; (2) the way in which his relatives and connexions were concerned in his business ventures ; (3) the way in which they were connected with the East India Company. The full family trees may be found in *Family Notes, Harrison-Branfill*, 2nd edition, 1897, compiled by Edward Harrison, Esq, for private circulation. They must, however, be supplemented by notes based on more recent research in MS., *ut sup.*, in the possession of R. T. Berthon, Esq.

II. THE BRANFILL FAMILY IN THE EIGHTEENTH CENTURY

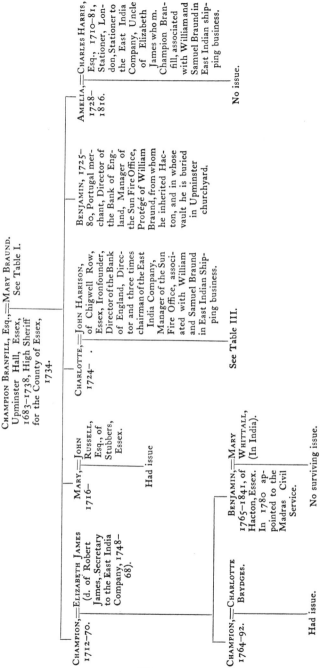

CHAMPION BRANFILL, Esq., = MARY BRAUND.
Upminster Hall, Essex,
1683–1738, High Sheriff
for the County of Essex,
1734.

See Table I.

CHAMPION, = ELIZABETH JAMES
1712–70. (d. of Robert
James, Secretary
to the East India
Company, 1748–
68).

MARY, = JOHN
1716– RUSSELL,
Esq., of
Stubbers,
Essex.

Had issue

CHARLOTTE, = JOHN HARRISON,
1724– . of Chigwell Row,
Essex, Ironfounder,
Director of the Bank
of England, Direc-
tor and three times
chairman of the East
India Company,
Manager of the Sun
Fire Office, associ-
ated with William
and Samuel Braund
in East Indian Ship-
ping business.

See Table III.

BENJAMIN, 1725–
80, Portugal mer-
chant, Director of
the Bank of Eng-
land, Manager of
the Sun Fire Office,
Protégé of William
Braund, from whom
he inherited Hac-
ton, and in whose
vault he is buried
in Upminster
churchyard.

AMELIA, = CHARLES HARRIS,
1728– Esq, 1710–81,
1816. Stationer, Lon-
don, Stationer to
the East India
Company, Uncle
of Elizabeth
James who m.
Champion Bran-
fill, associated
with William and
Samuel Braund in
East Indian ship-
ping business.

No issue.

CHAMPION, = CHARLOTTE
1764–92. BRYDGES.

Had issue.

BENJAMIN, = MARY
1765–1841, of WHITTALL,
Hacton, Essex. (In India).
In 1780 ap-
pointed to the
Madras Civil
Service.

No surviving issue.

11

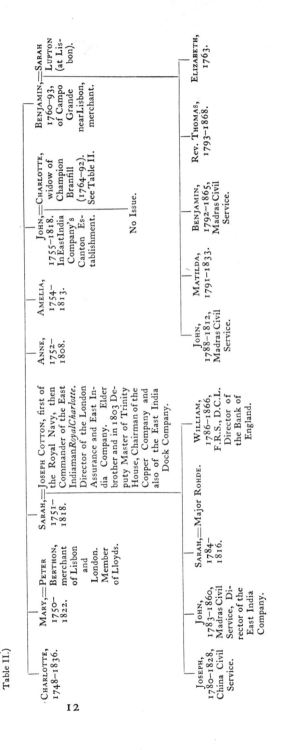

III. THE HARRISON FAMILY IN THE EIGHTEENTH CENTURY

BENJAMIN HARRISON,=SARAH DEANE, heiress to a family which c. 1694–1745, Surgeon and apothecary of Limehouse Corner, Stepney. seems to have had connexions with the East India Company. (Both were buried in the Deane Vault of the East India Company Chapel, Poplar.)

JOHN,=CHARLOTTE BRANFILL. 1721–94, of Chigwell Row, Essex. (See Table II.)

CHARLOTTE, 1748–1836.

MARY,=PETER BERTHON, 1750–1822. merchant of Lisbon and London. Member of Lloyds.

SARAH,=JOSEPH COTTON, first of the Royal Navy, then Commander of the East Indiaman *Royal Charlotte*. Director of the London Assurance and East India Company. Elder brother and in 1803 Deputy Master of Trinity House, Chairman of the Copper Company and also of the East India Dock Company. 1751–1818.

ANNE, 1752–1808.

AMELIA, 1754–1813.

JOHN,=CHARLOTTE, widow of Champion Branfill (1764–92). See Table II. 1755–1818. In East India Company's Canton Establishment.

No Issue.

BENJAMIN,=SARAH LUPTON (at Lisbon). 1760–93, of Campo Grande near Lisbon, merchant.

ELIZABETH, 1763.

JOSEPH, 1780–1828, China Civil Service.

JOHN, 1783–1860, Madras Civil Service, Director of the East India Company.

SARAH,=Major ROHDE. 1784–1816.

WILLIAM, 1786–1866, F.R.S., D.C.L. Director of the Bank of England.

JOHN, 1788–1812, Madras Civil Service.

MATILDA, 1791–1833.

BENJAMIN, 1792–1865, Madras Civil Service.

REV. THOMAS, 1793–1868.

12

Ministry took much of it over, to ministerial patronage itself.

The support which Braund obtained from family and neighbourhood was reinforced by that of purely business connexions. It was partly by his undoubtedly solid success and reputation for commercial integrity, but still more by the importance of certain connexions which he possessed in the City, that he gained the two distinctions he obtained there during his long life. He was for twenty-three years, from 1751 to 1774, a Manager of the Sun Fire Office, one of the three eighteenth-century fire insurance companies which gained so magnificent a tradition of soundness, and he was for eight years, from 1745 to 1753, a Director of the East India Company.[1] He held these positions as a representative of two overlapping groups. The former he entered as a member of the group of well-known merchants who dominated the Sun Fire Office, through his personal friendship, extending over many years of business relations, with one of the chief of them, Brice Fisher, a notable Blackwell-Hall factor,[2] who supplied him with cloths for the Portugal trade. He entered the East India Direction as a representative of the 'shipping interest', the closely organized monopoly of the East India 'ships' husbands' to which his brother Samuel belonged. He entered it, moreover, as the representative of a yet closer connexion, the group of part-owners (many of them influential in East Indian affairs) of the East Indiamen in which, either with Samuel or alone, he was interested. Here the most important figure was Richard Chauncey, Director of the East India Company from 1737 to 1754, Chairman in 1748, 1750, and 1753, who supplied a number of East Indiamen with gunpowder.[3] Here too, however, Brice

[1] C. C. Prinsep, *Record of Services of the Honorable East India Company's Civil Servants in the Madras Presidency from 1741 to 1858 . . . &c.*, 1885. (Including a list of directors.)

[2] L. B. Namier, *E. H. R.*, vol. xlii, p. 514. 'Brice Fisher M.P.: A mid-Eighteenth Century Merchant and his Connexions.'

[3] His trade in gunpowder was carried out in partnership with one Thomas Vigne. Richard Chauncey was the son of a prominent mining adventurer and the uncle of Chauncey Townsend, M.P. He appears in the merchant directories as a linen-draper. See L. B. Namier, *England in the Age of the American Revolution*, p. 284.

Fisher and his group, including the important American merchant Sir William Baker,[1] his business associate, were concerned. Not only were they shipowners, but Fisher was one of the factors through whom the Company bought its cloths for export, and as such he recognized, as the sequel suggests, the value of friends in the Direction of the Company.

These connexions gave Braund positions of distinction in the City, but they also involved him in the one scandal in which he ever seems to have been concerned. Braund was no doubt a man of integrity, trusted by all, the self-evident executor and trustee for his whole family, but his commercial morality was not above that of his age, and that morality reached its nadir in the affairs of the East India Company. His brother Benjamin, the Commander of the *Cumberland*, had been fined £100 by the Company for smuggling.[2] He himself was, only too openly, a 'shipping director', and, though the Company's by-laws explicitly forbade the directors to have part shares in ships in the Company's service, he not only remained during his term of office in the closest business relations with his brother Samuel, the ship's husband, but continued to be part owner of four East Indiamen. It was his relations with Brice Fisher, however, which brought him, though indirectly, into discredit. Though the most corrupt period of East India Company affairs did not begin till the 'sixties, these preceding years, in their more petty way, were almost as bad. It was in 1754 that it was discovered that quantities·of cloth had been delivered to the Company of a quality under sample.[3] The cloth was bought through Brice Fisher, and at least two of his group, Richard Chauncey and William Braund, had been members of the Committee of Buying at the time. It was alleged, moreover, though denied by those concerned, that Chauncey had told another member of the Committee 'You must buy these five hundred pieces'. Chauncey, who was still on the Direction, obtained a vote

---

[1] For Sir William Baker see L. B. Namier, *England in the Age of the American Revolution*, pp. 280 seq.

[2] India Office : E. I. Co., Ct. Bk. 54, f. 102, 26 Aug. 1730.

[3] India Office : E. I. Co., Ct. Bk. 66, f. 153 seq.   See Appendix I.

of exoneration from the charge, though the atmosphere of the Court was clearly suspicious; William Braund, who was, according to by-law, standing down for a year, came and gave evidence, and the clerk of the Committee was interrogated in his presence. Afterwards Thomas Burfoot, a packer, also one of the connexion, gave evidence and was cross-examined. Finally, the clothiers were forbidden to sell to the Company, and a motion to censure Brice Fisher for culpable negligence was only withdrawn when on ballot the voting was equal in favour and against. It is significant that neither Chauncey nor Braund stood for re-election next year, and that Brice Fisher sold no more cloths to the East India Company. It was a scandal, even in the East India Company, where scandals were common, and was the one blot on Braund's commercial record. Though he remained an owner of East Indiamen he never played any part in the Company's affairs again, and after the speculative disturbances in India Stock in 1766–7 did not even retain the £500 necessary for a vote, although John Harrison, his friend and the husband of his niece, was a prominent director who would, no doubt, have been glad of that vote. Very probably he deplored the whole course of East India affairs, for he seems to have agreed with the party Harrison supported in viewing with suspicion the policy of territorial conquest which Clive had inaugurated.

William Braund then stands before us, a man of substance, a Director of the East India Company, a member of the Sun Fire group of merchants to which such men as Brice Fisher belonged, of a family of merchants, ships' husbands, and ships' captains. His career seems to have been an illustration of that of many respectable merchants of his time. It has been remarked that the careers of all prominent London merchants of the mid-eighteenth century show a trend from commercial pursuits proper to those of pure finance,[1] as the great credit expansion of the eighteenth century, the last stage of the mobilization of commercial capital, opened new ways before them. Within its limits Braund's career shows the same tendency.

[1] L. B. Namier, *E. H. R.*, loc. cit.

Though he never speculated,[1] even in the East India Company—and though he did not grow rich on contracts and on contact with the treasury and its loans, yet his activities shifted none the less. From the time the accounts open, when he was already forty-six, until 1756, he divided his activities between underwriting and that wholesale exportation of woollens to Portugal which was the chief of his interests. He had also some ventures in ship-owning. From 1763 until his retirement from business in 1771 and even until his death in 1774, he was still interested in ship-owning, but otherwise confined himself to an increased business in marine underwriting. From 1756 to 1763 the transition between the two stages of his commercial career, his withdrawal from the ranks of the merchant proper took place under cover of his sudden and extensive venture in the Portuguese bullion trade, which together with his growing marine insurance took up during the Seven Years' War the full force of his energies and materially enlarged his fortunes. His Portuguese trade, first in the export of woollens, then in the import of gold bullion; his marine insurance in the formative years of Lloyd's Coffee-house; and his ship-owning, especially that which brought him into that most interesting monopoly, the 'shipping interest' of the East India Company, are the three main subjects treated in this study; for they serve to give from different angles some view of commercial London in the age of the dominance of commerce, and to justify the study of a merchant so soberly obscure as William Braund.

[1] For his investments see Appendix II.

II

THE PORTUGUESE VENTURES OF
WILLIAM BRAUND

THE greater part of William Braund's life was spent in the Portugal trade; it is to his activities there that we therefore turn first. The English trade with Portugal held a singular place in the practice and theory of English foreign trade for the first sixty years of the eighteenth century. It satisfied every requirement of mercantile economic theory. England exported to Portugal large quantities of her greatest products, woollens and worsteds, cloths, long ells, serges, tammies, and particularly 'our very great article of long bays'.[1] She shipped them almost entirely in her own bottoms, for Portuguese shipping was little developed in European waters. They were sent from the merchants in England to their correspondents, also English, in the factory at Lisbon; the latter distributed them to the Portuguese retailers or merchants, who tapped in their turn a still larger market, that of Spain or the Portuguese colony of Brazil. In part return England took port, an import which the strictest mercantile theorist could not oppose since it competed only with the clarets and burgundies of the 'hereditary enemy' France. Moreover, since the port, and other less valuable exports, failed altogether to make up Portugal's balance of trade, she was forced, though against all her own laws, to make up that balance by the export of the gold bullion she derived from the mines of Brazil. This fact in itself was enough to make a deep impression on contemporary opinion, which remained, for all the caustic criticisms levelled at the bullionist policies of Spain and Portugal, strictly bullionist. 'Gold in handling will stick to the Fingers like Meal,'[2] the Ministry was told in 1766 by Joseph Salvador, one of the shrewdest financiers of the time.

Every aspect of economic nationalism was therefore

---

[1] Mercator's *Letter on Portugal and its Commerce*, 1754. Note that this letter is reproduced verbatim under the title *Portugal* in M. Postlethwayt, op. cit., under the heading 'A Short Account of the Commerce of Portugal as lately given us on a very Interesting Occasion'.

[2] Brit. Mus. Add. MS. 38339, f. 225 v.

satisfied in this fortunate trade, and its encouragement
by the Government seemed a natural and laudable policy.
The Methuen Treaty of 1703, whereby the Portuguese
monarchy gave entry to all English woollens in return for
preference to its own port, was one of the most admired
successes of English diplomacy in the eighteenth century.
The popularity of the Portuguese trade did not wane till
after the mid-century. Then, through the competition of
France, felt as early as 1735 and strong by 1754, the sale
of English woollens was so much diminished that the
balance of trade was no longer for them, and the flow
of bullion stopped. As Mr. Lipson points out, the trade
treaty of Pitt with France in 1786, which has been hailed
as the herald of free trade, was due on the English side
less to a growing economic liberalism based on sympathy
with the doctrines of Adam Smith than to the loss of the
raison d'être of differentiation against France, the valuable
trade with Portugal.[1]

William Braund's connexion with Portugal covers, however, only the prosperous years of the trade. His ventures
are singularly interesting since they cover two separate
aspects of it, the woollen export trade and the trade in the
import of bullion. The former must have been the more
important to him, but the latter is of more significance to
us, for we know much of the organization of the woollen
trade but scarcely anything of that of the growing English
trade in bullion.

It is Braund's ventures in the bullion trade and its direct
development out of his woollen exportation to Portugal
which will therefore be studied here. It is an episode complete in itself and interesting in several ways. In the first
place it is an illustration of one of the means by which
the exporting merchant dominated English commerce and
adapted himself to its development, that is, through sheer
mobility and the poise of a purely intermediary position.
For Braund had neither store nor warehouse nor any stock
to put into them, nor did he ever play a part other than a
financier's in any of his trading activities at home. In his
foreign trade he bought woollens when he thought fit to

[1] E. Lipson, *The Economic History of England*, vol. iii, pp. 113–14.

send a consignment to Lisbon, had them dyed, packed, and dispatched by other firms, and received the profits of the transaction in due course. Braund was not one of those commercial aristocrats, the general merchants, nor could he claim to be what Adam Smith called a 'speculative' merchant, who 'enters into every trade when he foresees that it is likely to be more than commonly profitable, and ... quits it when he foresees that its profits are likely to return to the level of other trades '.[1] Still less had he the supreme position of 'the most skilful and vigilant merchant', the Napoleon of commerce, who could be either particular or general merchant 'particular ... generally, and general ... occasionally'.[2] Yet when circumstances suggested to him, as they did in 1756, that a new course of trade would be more profitable, it was no great matter for him to change from exporter to importer, from dealer in woollen goods to dealer in bullion.

In the second place, this episode serves as an individual illustration of one of the obscurest trades of eighteenth-century England. What William Braund was doing from 1756 to 1763, when he ceased to export woollen goods and began to bring gold to England and to tranship gold to the great banking firm of Cliffords in Amsterdam, was being done continually and in the same way by others, and no doubt often on a bigger scale; collectively they were building up a position for England in the bullion distri-bution of the world which played its part in the rise of London's money-market.

The obscurity in which the bullion trade of the eighteenth century has remained is not due to its lack of importance : it is due partly no doubt to the fact that the period was not, until cut across by the Napoleonic Wars, one of great price movement, partly to the fact that it was by the develop-ment of credit rather than the exploitation of new metallic sources that it met its growing commercial needs, but more to the fact that the conditions of the trade and its extent were veiled by a certain secrecy which political causes made desirable.[3] For, much as conditions had changed, the

---

[1] Op. cit. i. 115.   [2] M. Postlethwayt, op. cit., s.v. 'Mercantile College'.
[3] The force of this necessity was strongly brought out, for instance, in the

bullion supplies of the world remained chiefly those which Spain and Portugal controlled in South America, and the function of the trade in precious metals was still their more or less illegal distribution. While the centre of this distribution had been in the sixteenth century the centralized markets of Antwerp and the Genoese fairs, and their place had been taken in the seventeenth century by Amsterdam, in the eighteenth century circumstances were favouring in several ways the growing organization of London.[1] For one thing the great increase of Portuguese gold which followed the development of the Brazil mines at the end of the seventeenth century began to pass largely through English hands, on account of Portugal's commercial dependence on England. By 1750 England was admittedly the importer of the major part of the gold which, however checked, had to flow out of Portugal to pay for her imports. The importance of this factor in the commercial alliance between England and Portugal cannot be over-estimated.[2] For another thing, there developed in the silver trade at the beginning of the eighteenth century a new and more direct supply, through the contraband trade of the Spanish-American colonies with the foreign West Indies and mainland settlements. This trade, which became very extensive, fell largely into English hands. [3]

discussions with regard to the Spanish American bullion in 1764–6. Compare, for example, Brit. Mus. Add. MS. 33030, f. 189 seq.: Evidence before the House of Commons of Beeston Long of his interview with Grenville.

[1] The whole organization of the Bank of Amsterdam was, however, so arranged as to give every advantage to the City's great bullion trade. For a contemporary account see Adam Smith, *Wealth of Nations* (ed. Cannan), i. 443 seq. His information came from Henry Hope, a member of a prominent Amsterdam firm.

[2] Compare *The British Merchant*, Ed. C. King, 1721, ii. 24, iii. 19–20, &c. See J-G. Van Dillen, 'Amsterdam Marché Mondial des Métaux Précieux au XVIIe et au XVIIIe Siècle', in *Revue Historique*, July 1926, p. 194.

[3] The recent development of this trade was brought out in the discussions from 1764 to 1766 of its place in the provisions of the Navigation Acts (v. Brit. Mus. Add. MS. 32971, f. 16 v., Memorandum, n.d. [late 1765]: The Advice of Mr. —— to the Ministry). 'When the Statute of the 7th and 8th of King William was made Mr. —— doth not believe the practice of the Spaniards bringing Bullion to the said Dominions, to lay out in goods and Manufactures, had then begun .... Mr. —— believes, that the Practice of the Spaniards remitting Bullion to Great Britain did not take place till many years after the passing of the Act.' Despite the fears of N. Magens (*Universal Merchant*, 1753, p. 15), that the trade was being lost and passing into French hands, the Bullion Report of 1810 (E. Cannan, *The Paper Pound*) mentions this trade as one of first-class importance.

In the ordinary course of her trade, then, England was obtaining increased supplies of precious metals, which she required the more as her East Indian trade, and the silver export which it necessitated, were increasing. Still further, however, her transactions were now increased by her importance as a transhipper of gold and silver for other nations. In the Portuguese trade it was said, as Beawes stresses in his *Lex Mercatoria Rediviva*, that shipments of gold were made directly to Italy alone, but to all other nations through England ' on account of the conveniency of the Exchange and of shipping'.[1] In the Spanish South American trade in silver[2] an even more striking development was seen, for here England actually transhipped silver for Spain herself. A financial adviser told the English Government :

' A vast quantity of Bullion hath been sent for many years last past to His Majesty's Dominions in America, not to be laid out there, but to be sent to Great Britain to make remittances, or on freight only for the use of the Spaniards, with a design to avoid the heavy indultus of 12 and sometimes more per cent. on Bullion and other charges remitted to Spain, by which the senders gain as circumstances vary from 8 to 10 or 13 per cent.'[3]

The development of the market in London to deal with this increased flow of bullion was considerable. Its central feature was, of course, the rise to predominance of the Bank of England as a buyer of bullion. By 1765 it was stated that into its hands ' almost all comes '.[4] Some houses of goldsmith bullion merchants, however, kept up an independent position. George Masterman, goldsmith, giving evidence before the House of Commons in 1766, as one of the chief buyers of silver bullion in Lombard Street, stated

[1] p. 624.

[2] It centred chiefly in Jamaica. Interesting returns were made by the Bank of England at the command of the House of Commons in January 1766 of the silver imports from the British American Colonies, 1748–65. (Brit. Mus. MS. 32971, f. 64 seq.) The following are the total imports for these years :

Jamaica, £2,368,484.	Virginia, £22,750.
Other West Indies, £20,826.	South Carolina, £23,200.
Havannah, £559,110.	Quebec, £20,000.
New York, £171,782.	Not distinguished, £69,504.

[3] Brit. Mus. Add. MS. 32971, f. 16, n.d. [1765]: Opinion of Mr. ——.

[4] Brit. Mus. Add. MS. 38339, f. 225, 28 Jan. 1766 : Joseph Salvador, the Jewish financier.

that as much as £320,000 of American silver passed through his house in the years 1761–5, and maintained that he could not put himself 'at the Head' of his trade.[1] The position he describes is not essentially different from that described in 1810 by Goldsmid of Mocatta and Goldsmid, bullion brokers to the Bank of England, except that the private buyers seem to have still had a somewhat more prominent position then than they maintained later.[2] His evidence makes it clear that it was customary for the ships' captains, both merchantmen and men-of-war, to take bullion directly either to a goldsmith banker or to the Bank.

The Bullion Office, or Warehouse as it was called until the end of the eighteenth century, where this bullion was received, was said to have existed almost since the Bank's institution 'for the purpose of accommodation and safety between merchant and merchant, as a place of deposit'.[3] Masterman mentions that 'all Captains of Men of War make it a rule to go to the Bank of England', but that merchantmen sometimes preferred to take the bullion to a goldsmith buyer, who kept what he wanted himself, and 'carried to the Bank' the rest. This method, very convenient for the importer, explains why there is only the one entry of each bullion import in the Braund books, an entry with freight deducted, and why there is no trace of any method of handling or disposing of the gold. The methods of a merchant transhipping gold for a correspondent to another foreign centre through the London market are illustrated by the Braund accounts. Two transactions were involved. All bullion entering from Portugal for this purpose was credited to the correspondent with the other shipments intended for Braund himself, and was

---

[1] T. Mortimer, *The Universal Director*, 1763, mentions a firm, How and Masterman, goldsmiths, of White-Hart Court, Gracechurch Street. F. G. Hilton Price, *Handbook of London Bankers*, has found no reference to a Masterman as goldsmith or banker earlier than 1780, when the firm of Mildred, Masterman, and Walker, of Lombard Street, is mentioned.

George Masterman's evidence is found in rough notes among the Newcastle Papers (Brit. Mus. Add. MS. 33030, f. 148 seq.).

[2] *Reports &c., from Committees of the House of Commons*, 1810, vol. iii, p. 35. Minutes of Evidence before the 'Bullion Committee'.

[3] Ibid., p. 146. Evidence of J. Humble, Clerk in the Bullion Office of the Bank of England.

thus paid for in the usual way. Thus, to carry out the commission Braund bought bullion to the amount specified in foreign coin and shipped it to the recipient as if it were a private venture, receiving in due course from him repayment in bill of exchange from Amsterdam.

The buying and selling required some skill and foresight, and was placed by Malachy Postlethwayt among the most skilled branches of the great 'art of merchandising', though so wide a knowledge of 'the markets where and seasons when it is to be bought cheap and sold . . . dear',[1] as he assumes, was more necessary for a skilled arbitrageur than a simple importer such as William Braund became. Nevertheless, not only were his problems those which required knowledge of the exchanges, and an understanding of the imperfection of the normal arbitrage activities of his time, but they were further complicated by the unstable eighteenth-century bimetallism, by a market in gold disordered by depreciation of the currency, and by the prohibition of the export of English coin. Thus during the eight years of Braund's activities in bullion dealing the price of gold fluctuated from £3 17s. to £4 1s. 2d. per standard ounce,[2] and Malachy Postlethwayt, in his tables for the calculation of the value of precious metals of all degrees of purity, gives figures for silver from the price of 5s. to that of 5s. 6⅞d. per standard ounce, and for gold from £3 15s. 6d. to £4 1s.[3]

The trade which William Braund carried on with Portugal, at first in woollens and then in bullion, was organized according to the manner of his time, and it is significant of that time that his change in trade from one commodity to another was effected without the need of any marked alteration in the methods or channels of his business. Throughout, his trade was carried on through a firm of merchants living in one of the foreign factories in Lisbon,

---

[1] Op. cit., 'Bullion'.
[2] The causes are analysed in the Bullion Report of 1810 (*The Paper Pound*, E. Cannan).
[3] Op. cit., s.v. 'Bullion'. A distinction must be made at this time between the price of gold in foreign coin, in which Braund dealt almost exclusively, and that of bar gold—the former always tending to be somewhat higher than the latter, on account of the greater demand for it abroad.—Bullion Report of 1810 (*The Paper Pound*, E. Cannan, p. 4).

who acted as his agents or factors ; as importing agents in the first period of his activities they received his shipments of woollens and distributed them, generally on long credit, to Portuguese tradesmen or merchants ; later, as exporting agents, they bought and dispatched his gold for him to England. Such agents were rarely Portuguese, for, as contemporaries said, with fine trading scorn, 'The Portuguese carry on no active commerce . . . they buy everything from foreigners settled in factories there '.[1] In 1741, when Braund's accounts begin, and when his activities, less concentrated than later, included relations with firms in Holland,[2] he appears to have been employing as agent in Lisbon a Dutch firm, Schutte, Buess, and Renner. After 1743, however, no transactions with them are recorded in his journal, though old debts are sent by them through his new agents for some years. In his choice of new agents Braund was more orthodox, for he chose a firm in the English factory, Jackson and Carse. Still more characteristic of the commercial habits of the time was the fact that his nephew Benjamin Branfill, shortly after the connexion began, entered the firm as a junior partner. The firm stands finally in Braund's great ledger under the name of Jackson, Branfill, and Goddard.[3]

The relations between Braund and Jackson, Branfill and Goddard were complicated, but not, it seems probable, uncommon. The Lisbon house cannot be put under the category of either agent, commission house, or branch firm.[4] The connexion was more than the simple one of agent and principal, for there was the close relationship of kin, and an equally close one of credit. In 1758 the firm owed Braund £12,500 on its own account, in addition to a personal debt of his nephew, Benjamin Branfill.[5] Jackson, Branfill, and Goddard was not, on the other hand, a branch firm, for Braund had not founded it, and a relationship

---

[1] Mercator, op. cit. This taunt, never altogether justified, ceased to be true at all after the formation in 1756 by Pombal of the Companies of Brazil and the Alto Douro.   [2] J. Daniel Baur, and Tempelman's widow and Kroeger.

[3] Goddard's name first appears in the accounts in Sept. 1754.

[4] R. B. Westerfield, op. cit., p. 351.

[5] Benjamin Branfill owed his uncle personally in 1758 £1,561 19s. 11d. The debt of the firm appears in that year to have been written down to half.

similar to that with Braund appears also to have existed with another London merchant, Philip Jackson, whose name first appears in 1753, and who was, presumably, a relative of the Jackson of the Portuguese firm.[1] The use of branch firms was in the Portuguese trade, as in other kinds of distant commerce, indeed a common method of seeking to evade the very real dangers of careless or fraudulent agents; but it seems probable that many of the well-known names—such as Bristow, Ward & Co., the agents of John Bristow of London; Burrell, Duckett, and Hardy, the agents of Burrell and Raymond;[2] and Chase, Wilson & Co., the agents of T. Chase—had a more independent existence than that of branch firms proper. Nor can Jackson, Branfill, and Goddard be regarded, finally, as a pure commission house; for though it carried on 'commission business' for Philip Jackson and Braund, and, the accounts seem to suggest, for another London merchant, Thomas Godfrey, it also carried on its own independent trade, as its bullion ventures were later to show. It is more proper to consider it as one of those firms of 'the highest credit throughour Europe' whose custom it was 'to act mutually in the capacity of factors to each other',[3] but one that had close relations with, and possibly even some dependence on Braund and other English merchants.

Braund's transactions through Jackson, Branfill, and Goddard can be examined in four different account books: his great Ledger F, 'the grand and principal book of account',[4] covering the years 1758–65;[5] his Fair Journal, which also begins only in 1758; his Rough Journal, with its daily entries under separate accounts, which runs from 1741 to 1764 (with, however, an unexplained gap from

---

[1] Philip Jackson, merchant, of Charterhouse Yard, appears first in Kent's Directory in 1754, and his name continues there until the issue of 1774. He was Director and Deputy-Governor of the South Sea Company. He is among the signatories of a petition of Portuguese merchants to the Board of Trade and Plantations, 15th May 1756. P.R.O. C.O. 388/48, ff. 16 seq. See Appendix II.

[2] The position is here further complicated by the fact that Burrell and Bristow of London were, for a good deal of their business at least, in partnership.

[3] M. Postlethwayt, op. cit., s.v. 'Factors'.

[4] Ibid. op. cit., s.v. 'Mercantile Accountantship'.

[5] Two ledgers only have survived, F and G, the latter of which runs from 1765 to Braund's death in 1774.

1745 to 1749 inclusive); and his Cash Book, which runs
from 1747 to 1774, thus covering, though not by its nature completely, the later years of the gap in the journal.[1]
Trading relations between the two firms evidently began
during the years of this gap, for the first evidence which
we have of them is a note in the cash book of a bill of
exchange from Jackson and Carse on 9 December 1747.
During the remaining two years before the resumption of
the journal there is no evidence of the trade except such
receipts of bills of exchange. Their annual totals :

	£	s.	d.
1747 (August to December only)	470	3	1
1748	1,490	6	10
1749	3,523	1	7

although they cannot, owing to the use of long credit, be held
to represent the value of the consignments of woollen goods
for the year in which the payment occurs, suggest at least
a growing trade.

By 1750, however, both sides of the transactions are
before us, and, though only the ledger could make clear
the entire position, the extent and methods of trade can
be examined in detail; for Braund clearly supported the
current commercial maxim that 'in journalizing the waste
book lies all the difficulty of account-keeping',[2] and his
journal is full and methodical. An examination of his
trade from 1750 onwards shows that the volume of his exportation for the next five years was, like that of England
as a whole, fluctuating but not increasing; and that in its
organization as in its extent it had become very systema-
tized. Except in unusual circumstances every consignment
of woollens was entered in two forms, first as a debit to
'Voyage to Lisbon', when the 'first cost' and 'charges'
were entered; later, after varying intervals, as a debit to
Jackson, Branfill, and Goddard, when the 'net price' was
given, the sum for which they disposed of the goods to
Portuguese merchants, less freight, customs, and warehouse
charges. This method has the convenience of enabling a calculation to be made of the profit or loss of each transaction.

---

[1] The cash book has no record of shipments of woollens or of charges.
[2] M. Postlethwayt, op. cit., s.v. 'Mercantile Accountantship'.

The 'first cost' was the price actually paid by Braund for the materials. They consisted of various types of woollens, some cloths and serges, but the greater part worsteds and semi-worsteds such as shalloons, tammies, long ells, and in particular long bays. He obtained the materials from three of the different sources opened to the merchant buyer by the complicated machinery of the distribution of the woollen trade.[1] The most important among them was his packer, Thomas Burfoot, who, like many packers and warehousemen of the time, had evolved from his packing business a very considerable position as a merchant.[2] Burfoot, who had connexions with a firm of woollen drapers in Cornhill, Burfoot and Ellis, not only packed all Braund's goods but supplied him with most of the long ells which he required, occasionally undertook some of his dyeing (presumably having it done elsewhere), and was, at least on one occasion, the intermediary through whom he bought his blankets. When Braund gave up the woollen trade, his name is one of the few which is still to be found in the accounts, for he then began to appear as the drawer of numerous bills of exchange on a Portuguese firm in Lisbon.[3] The rise of such extra intermediaries in the woollen trade was deplored by merchant and clothier alike, but really was an essential condition of the mobility and power of the exporting merchant. The second of Braund's sources was also a type, and a very notable one, of London intermediary, the Blackwell-Hall factor. From a well-known man among them, Brice Fisher,[4] with whom he had other relations as well, Braund obtained all the broadcloth which he exported. In the same way he purchased his coatings from the well-known firm of London warehousemen and merchants, Samuel and Thomas Fludyer,[5] and for shalloons

---

[1] Cf. E. Lipson, *History of the English Woollen and Worsted Industries*, 1921 H. Heaton, op. cit.

[2] R. B. Westerfield, op. cit., pp. 312–13.

[3] Thomas Burfoot. He is to be found at the same warehouse in Bucklersbury in the Directories from 1736 to 1776. In 1759 the firm appears as Thomas Burfoot and Son; from 1774 to 1776 as Burfoot and Bristow.

[4] Brice Fisher. See above, p. 13.

[5] Samuel and Thomas Fludyer. This distinguished firm (Thomas was knighted, and Samuel was made a baronet and was in 1761 Lord Mayor of London) is throughout Kent's Directory described as a firm of warehousemen. They

he relied chiefly on a very solid and long-established London firm, Jeremiah, John, and Robert Royd, who are described in Kent's *Directory* of 1754 as 'Yorkshire Factors' but in T. Mortimer's *Universal Director* of 1763 as 'Norwich Warehousemen'. His third source was local merchants. His tammies were obtained chiefly from Thomas Humphreys, who does not appear to have been a London merchant, and the needs of his great exportation of long bays were almost entirely met by one Thomas Ruggles of Bocking, with whom, moreover, he carried on for some years a joint inland trade.[1]

The woollens when bought were undyed and in the case of the tammies unscoured, and, since Braund had no warehouses, were dispatched directly to the firms of dyers and packers, whose payment makes up the item of 'charges'. The proportion of these charges to the 'first cost' was often very high, sometimes almost half as much again, and it is noticeable that in almost every case Braund makes in his entries a small but varying addition to their total, presumably the small increment, varying from 5 per cent. to 10 per cent. or even more, which, as Postlethwayt notes, merchants were accustomed to add to the prices of goods sent to their agents, 'especially if the goods happen to be well-bought'.[2] Braund dealt regularly with three firms of dyers, John Spence, Owen Larton, and Thomas Maryatt, whose place was later taken by Roberts and Kinleside. Thomas Burfoot, the only packer employed,

traded widely, however, as West India merchants and were generally designated as such. In fact, Thomas Mortimer in his *Universal Director* of 1763 includes them as West India merchants in a work which is specifically intended to enable 'foreigners to avoid dealing with warehousemen who call themselves Merchants, whereas their proper business is to supply the Retailer'. On the Fludyers cf. L. B. Namier, *England in the Age of the American Revolution*, pp. 254 n., 281-2.

[1] The account for trade in company with Thomas Ruggles closes in 1759, and in 1760 there is a note of cash received from his executors. The sums paid to profit and loss on this account show that for the last three years at least this trade was very small:

1757	. .	£30 8s. 0d.
1758	. .	£35 9s. 5d.
1759	. .	£11 6s. 9d.

These sums, together with £500 carried over from the preceding ledger, were paid by Ruggles in 1759. Somewhat scattered earlier references to the trade show it to have been much bigger before.

[2] M. Postlethwayt. op. cit., s.v. 'Factors'.

was presumably also the shipper. Since the freights were paid in Lisbon, and deducted from the net price owed by the agents there, the accounts give no information as to their amounts,[1] but they show that the goods were consigned, as was to be expected, in English ships, with only one exception, and that among the ships' names which constantly recur are two in which Braund had an owner's share, as he had later in one of the packet boats which shipped his bullion.

The fluctuation in the bulk of the exports, which was probably occasioned among other things by the slowness and uncertainty with which the agents were able to distribute them, is illustrated by the following table of bales exported, and their cost:

Date	No. of Bales	Cost		
		£	s.	d.
1750	109	7,694	13	1
1751	29	1,836	5	10
1752	81	4,047	19	8
1753	86	5,453	6	6
1754	101	7,127	16	3
1755 (an abnormal year)	127	8,300	16	10

The remittances in payment for the woollens show none of this irregularity, for the long credit necessary in this trade prevented their having any close relations with the amount of the consignments. The accounts bring out in this connexion some important facts with regard to the exchange between England and Portugal. Though the exchange was notoriously and necessarily against Portugal during the greater part of this time, the payments never took the form of bullion, until Braund became an importer

---

[1] An illustration occurs in these accounts of freights from Holland in 1741 :

	£	s.	d.
Paid feci (*sic*) of entry of 8 sacks of Estridge Wool (i.e. ostrich down) per Two Brothers		4	6
Wharfidge and Lighteridge 16s., Porters Landing 8s.	1	4	0
Land waiters 8s. Cartidge 9s. 6d.		17	6
Freight and primidge	19	10	0
	21	16	0

[primage was a customary perquisite of the captain. Commonly 5 per cent. of freight (Beawes, *Lex Mercatoria Rediviva*, 1752, p. 142).]

of precious metals, but always that of bills of exchange, primarily Portuguese trading bills, many of them drawn by agents on their English correspondents in connexion no doubt with the wine trade. This consistent remittance of payments by bill makes clear another point; for they show that there could exist a very marked discrepancy between the levels on the London and the Lisbon bill-markets. In London the milreis generally stood below gold export point—5*s*. 6·01*d*.,[1] a position characteristic of the exchange on a country whence gold is exported as a commodity, while in Lisbon it might, and usually did, stand at the same time from 5*s*. 6·25*d*. to 5*s*. 7*d*. The explanation lay primarily, no doubt, in the risk created by the prohibition of the export of gold, though the seriousness of this risk varied greatly. It is significant, however, that just the reverse position existed at the end of the eighteenth century between England and Hamburg. Nathan Rothschild attributed it largely to the fact that, as the exchange tended to be fixed at Hamburg, merchants there bought bills for investment, and

'sending them to London to get returns: they have, therefore to take into their calculation the amount of interest on the bills so sent, as well as those received in return, together with two brokerages, and a commission to the London Merchant.'[2]

It seems probable that this factor of investment played its part in the opposite way in the Lisbon-London exchange.

A comparison of 'first costs' and 'charges' with 'net prices' shows the profits of the trade. Taking 1753 as a more or less representative year,[3] we see that Braund gained on an outlay of £5,462 13*s*. 8*d*. a profit of £564 6*s*. 4*d*., about 10⅓ per cent., a satisfactory return and above Adam Smith's 'good, moderate, reasonable profit', for it was

---

[1] So taken from official sources by V. M. Shillington and A. B. Chapman, *The Commerical Relations of England and Portugal*, p. 290 n. *The British Merchant* (ed. 1721), iii. 108, quoted without correction by Postlethwayt, op. cit. (s.v. 'Exchange'), states that it was under 5*s*. 6*d*.

[2] *Reports, &c., from Committees of the House of Commons*, 1810, iii. 73–4. Evidence before the 'Bullion Committee' of Mr. —— , to be identified in all probability, as has been suggested (*The Paper Pound*, E. Cannan, p. xlii), with Nathan Rothschild.

[3] See table.

more than 'double interest',[1] though it must be remembered that credit was long, and, as the sequel showed, bad debts common.

Such was the nature of Braund's commerce with Portugal, which had gone on for years and might have gone on unchanged for many more. On 1 November 1755, however, there came upon it, with shattering effects, the great Lisbon earthquake, which temporarily paralysed the commercial activities of the whole of Portugal. The earthquake and its sequels affected Braund both in his own trade and in that of the country. In his own trade he suffered personal losses, through goods burned in the customs house, no doubt through ruined customers, and, it would appear, through the shaken credit of his agents.[2] It is significant that he should, within three months, have closed down his old account with them, and that for the next eight years they were repaying personal debts incurred by them for the most part, if not entirely, before the earthquake. It was clear also that a shock had been given to the woollen trade in general at a time when, in any case, as the next twenty years were to show, it was meeting new and adverse conditions.[3] At first, it was true, as soon as the immediate dislocation of the earthquake was over there was a tem-

---

[1] Adam Smith, op. cit., i. 99. He also states that in England 'the ordinary profits of stock . . . are supposed to run between six and ten per cent.' (i. 293).

It is impossible to isolate the expenses which were incidental to Braund's Portuguese trade from those which he incurred for other purposes. As has been already pointed out, he had no warehouses, so they were not heavy.

[2] The English factory suffered severely in the earthquake. Abraham Castres, the British Envoy-Extraordinary, wrote to Sir Thomas Robinson (Brit. Mus. Add. MS. 32860, f. 382 v.) on 6 Nov. 1755, that they had 'for the most part lost all they had, tho' some, indeed, as Messrs. Purry and Mellish's House and Mr. Raymond and Burrell's have had the good Fortune to save their Cash, either in whole or in part'.

[3] A petition from the Portugal merchants, among whom was William Braund, was sent in to the Board of Trade and Plantations on 15 May 1756, in which they speak of 'their great and heavy losses upon this calamitous occasion (more than many could well bear)'. It was signed by sixty-three London merchants, and was supported by a letter from thirteen merchants of Norwich. (P.R.O. C.O. 388/48, ff. 16 seq.) See Appendix II.

C. Whitworth's tables (State of the Trade of Great Britian, 1776, part 2, p. 28), however, while they show a very heavy fall in imports from Portugal in 1756, show a large increase in exports to her, and no fall until 1758. Braund's accounts for 1756 would suggest that this increase was largely to meet the losses of the earthquake, and it is possible that, under the spur of the first high prices, the exportation of goods thither was overdone. The depression of 1758 was not permanent,

porary but acute scarcity of and demand for woollen goods. To meet this demand in November, Braund rushed out to his agents (apparently on what he called 'the New Account ') the largest shipment (81 bales) that he had ever sent, and in January another of considerable size. The profits which he obtained upon them, ranging from 16 per cent. to 67 per cent. indicate sufficiently the disorganized condition of trade in Portugal. But Braund was too shrewd not to realize that this was but a passing phase. After his shipment of January 1756 he sent only three bales for the rest of the year. In 1757 he sent only two; thence onward, his activities as a woollen exporter ceased altogether, never to be renewed. Already on 4 February 1756 there is the first entry in the accounts of a remittance from Jackson, Branfill, and Goddard in gold bullion; on 8 April there is the first mention of a new and separate account with them, 'the exchange account', and from that time on, with no change in the relations between the firms, and with little perceptible reorganization of Braund's resources, the old woollen export trade merges into a new bullion import one, a merging the more indistinguishable because part of the bullion remittances was in payment for old debts in wool. War-time conditions were soon to help the growing trade, for in May 1756 England declared war on France, and in August Frederick the Great invaded Saxony. The Seven Years' War had begun.

It was thus not the war which tempted Braund to show his adaptability and powers as 'a skilful and vigilant merchant', though, as the rising price of gold followed the needs of war, his ventures expanded greatly. What had determined his action was firstly the damage done to his trade in woollens, and secondly the increased profits in the bullion trade which followed the sudden movement of the exchanges against Portugal, already beneath gold point, after the disaster. That he was not alone in seizing the

Portugal beginning to share in the general war boom of Europe. The permanent depression did not come until after the peace.

The import of gold bullion from Portugal which made up the balance is, of course, not included in these figures, as no record was kept of its entry.

For the other conditions unfavourable to the Portugal trade at this time see E. Lipson, *The Economic History of England*, iii. 113–14.

opportunity is suggested by the occurrence in 1755 of one of the spasmodic attempts made by the Portuguese Government to check the smuggling of bullion out of the country. The increase of gold importation into England, moreover, in the years following 1756, was considerable enough to upset seriously the always unstable English bimetallism. The position of silver in relation to gold during the whole of the obscure development of England towards a virtually monometallic standard, was one of under-valuation, which, in any case, tended to leave none but the lighter coins in circulation. During periods of abnormal drain of silver or abnormal increase of gold, a real scarcity in silver, the chief internal currency of the country, took place. Such was the case during the succeeding years. Even in 1717, when it had been decided to lower the value of the guinea, it was only suggested as a possibility that the English would soon refuse to pay in silver except at a premium ' as they do in Spain ', but in 1759 Sir John Barnard stated that the payment of such a premium by the banks was a well-known fact.[1]

The first consignment of gold which Braund received in February 1756 was not, however, the beginning of a new trade, but a new means of payment for his old : the first occasion in which this method was employed in preference to that of bill of exchange ; and from that time on until the final closing of his old woollens accounts it continued to be

---

[1] Sir Isaac Newton, *Mint Reports* (1701–25), in *Select Tracts and Documents Illustrative of English Monetary History*, ed. W. A. Shaw, 1896. The Spanish premium was said to be generally 6 per cent. Sir John Barnard said in his *Some Thoughts on the Scarcity of Silver Coin : with a Proposal for Remedy thereof* (March 1759) : ' It is well known that the Bankers generally give a Premium for silver Coin to supply their Customers.' He had already written on the subject in the preceding May. In 1759 the position was aggravated by a heavy fall in the quantity of silver imported from the Spanish South American colonies, the Bank of England returns showing a fall in the imports from Jamaica from £76,900 in 1758 to £23,400 in 1759. The decline was only temporary. Brit. Mus. Add. MS. 32971, f. 64 : ' An Account of the Bullion Imported and Brought to the Bank from the several Colonies in North America from the Year 1748 to the Year 1765 both inclusive.' (Drawn up at the command of the House of Commons *Commons Journal*, vol. xxx. 500, 27 January 1766.) The evidence of W. Merle before the Bullion Committee of 1810 (*Reports, &c., from Committees of the House of Commons*, 1810, vol. iii. 54) states that bankers continued giving a premium for silver until the introduction of stamped dollars as currency, and at harvest time or other occasions of great scarcity sometimes did so since that time. The premium was said to be 1½ per cent.

used. The debts owing to him on this old trade can unfortunately only be seen in full when the ledger opens in 1758, almost two years after the woollen trade had ceased to be of importance to him. By that time a distinction between the 'old' and 'new' accounts (or 'woollens' as the latter begins to be called in contradistinction to 'exchange') first seen at the beginning of 1756, stood for the distinction between a debt owed by the agents personally, the 'old' account, and debts which they were collecting in their capacity of agents. On the first there was a heavy debt of £12,500 written down to half the sum,[1] on which annual repayments were made through Philip Jackson of London, but of which £681 remained unpaid when the account was finally closed. The method of repayment, and the final loss to Braund suggest that the firm of Jackson, Branfill, and Goddard had been so badly crippled by the earthquake, and possibly other misfortunes and mistakes, that they had, like Defoe's *Complete English Tradesman*, been 'wise enough, as well as honest enough, to break betimes',[2] and were during these years in composition with their creditors, but that the opening of the bullion trade had given them a renewed opportunity for 'commission business' and thus a renewed lease of life. On the new account there was also, in 1758, a heavy debt, £7,613 16s. 6d. The difficulties of collecting this debt are suggested by a note in the ledger:

'Debts out Standing the first of March 1762.

314Ұ235. Jono Texeira Macedo, will pay on the arrival of the Rio fleet.

995Ұ630. Balthasar Pinto de Miranda, to pay when he can Sell his Hides, lately accepted a considerable post in the New Treasury.[3]

222Ұ640. Jose Devarte Ferreira dead, but are assured his partner in the Rio will pay all his debts, expected by the next fleet.'

[1] So it would appear from the not very explicit entries in the ledger.
[2] Reprint of 1839, p. 43.
[3] This customer, however, later became bankrupt. Losses also occurred though having to accept payments in kind. In February 1763 there is the entry: 'Loss on my debt of 2,659Ұ140 of Bernardo Gomez Costa by taking Hydes . . . £49 16s. 7d.'

Nevertheless all but a small sum, £41 8s. 5d., was paid off by remittances in bullion between 1758 and 1763, remittances which came in side by side with the new trading imports.

While this repayment went on the trade in bullion gradually grew. Braund received remittances for two purposes, for his own use and for re-export to Holland; in the first he was the principal, in the second the agent, a new mutual relationship. The imports were distinguished from the remittances of debts by the fact that, while 1 per cent. commission was credited to the agent on the latter,[1] only ⅓ per cent. plus postage was allowed on the former, the same commission as Braund received on his re-exports to Holland. Brokerage on the bills of exchange and freight were paid by Braund himself and deducted from his profits.

In the first two years Braund's ventures were only tentative. The price of gold was still relatively low, fluctuating about £3 17s. 10½d. per standard ounce, and the effect of the Portuguese dislocation was not fully reflected in the exchanges until the beginning of 1757. In 1756 only four shipments of gold on the exchange account, worth £1,852 8s. 10d., were received by Braund, and two bills of exchange sent out, worth £920 16s. 8d. In 1757 there were again only four, for the value of £1,400 6s. 9d., though the price of gold had risen by the end of the year to £3 18s. 3d.; on the other hand, the extreme lowness of the exchange in England (about 5s. 4½d.) led Braund to much greater purchases of bills of exchange to further the trade, and ten are entered in the ledger, for the value of £2,778 7s. 3d. By 1758, when the price of gold was hovering between £3 18s. 1½d. and £3 19s. 3d., and was still rising, the trade was at its height. This period of zenith lasted from 1758 to 1761. With the needs of a European war, the price of gold rose to a peak in June 1761 of £4 1s. 2d., and even when the exchanges with Portugal rose above the normal gold export point, as they began to do during certain months of these years, the rising price of gold made its continued import profitable.

---

[1] M. Postlethwayt, op. cit., s.v. 'Factors', quotes 2 per cent. as the customary factorage in the Portuguese trade.

Braund's dealings during these years may be shown by the following figures:

Date.	Value of Bullion Imported.			Value of Bills of Exchange.		
	£	s.	d.	£	s.	d.
1758.	11,559	9	1	11,921	18	9
1759.	12,164	9	6	11,415	19	7
1760.	12,704	9	7	14,725	6	9
1761.	12,369	14	9	11,162	0	5
1762.	7,152	7	9	3,641	14	8
1763.	443	1	6			

The imports, with the exception of two remittances in silver,[1] were in gold, and were only on one occasion in bars, being for the rest in Portuguese coins.[2] Where possible they were shipped on one of the four packet boats, in one of which, the *Hanover*, Braund had an owner's share; otherwise they were sent by man-of-war, as no ship could be used for this smuggling trade which had not immunity from search. The advantage of the former was that the freight was charged at only ¼ per cent. of the value of the bullion, while on the latter it was 1 per cent.[3]

The bills of exchange in which payments for the remittances were made, were drawn from much more varied sources than those which had before been drawn from Lisbon in payment for the trade in woollens. They suggest the contrast between the importance of Lisbon and London as a financial centre and indicate both the organization of the London bill-market and its growing width. The majority of the bills which are entered in Braund's ledger are, indeed, as in the case of those drawn from Lisbon, drawn by merchants on their correspondents, as for instance those of Philip Jackson drawn on Jackson, Branfill, and Goddard themselves. Others, however, while still bills of prominent London merchants connected with the Portuguese trade, were clearly not ordinary trade bills. The bills drawn by Thomas Burfoot the packer, for instance, were

---

[1] Silver could be legally exported from Portugal by licence. Mercator, op. cit., says the licence was ' rarely or never sollicited '. Jackson, Branfill, and Goddard, however, obtained one for one of their two silver remittances.

[2] No doubt because the price of coins was higher.

[3] ' Carriage ' appears to be the word used for the packet boat, ' Freight ' only or man-of-war.

far too frequent and regular in their amounts to be the trading bills of a merchant. They are found almost monthly, usually for 1,000 milreis, from 1758 until early in 1762, when two of them were protested for non-payment, and the series abruptly ends. The circumstances clearly point to some arrangement for 'accommodation' bills such as the needs of the bullion trade called forth. That the mechanism was not, however, as elastic as it might have been, was shown by the fact that the market was sometimes strained beyond capacity by the demands made upon it in the course of the trade; for instance, in 1737 the influx of Portuguese gold through Falmouth caused serious inconvenience in the internal trade of England, for it engrossed all the bills of exchange from Cornwall to London.[1]

Apart, however, from such development of the organization of exchange made by London merchants themselves, there are signs of a very real development of the London bill-market, both in its national and international aspects.

Within England itself can be seen a fair sprinkling of bills on Portuguese correspondents from merchants in such country towns as Exeter, Leeds, and Norwich, for instance from the Gurneys, direct dealers in the cloth or wine trades, who worked independently of such London exporters as Braund had been. In drawing by bill of exchange on their correspondents, however, they could not maintain this independence, and the bills were in each case discounted by a London goldsmith banker, such as Coutts or Hoare. This followed logically from the centralization in the hands of such bankers of the internal bill system. In the sphere of international exchange, while Amsterdam was admittedly still the arbiter of the exchanges of Europe, it can be seen how the predominance of English trade to Portugal brought to the London bill-market bills from all countries of Europe. There are among those sent by Braund to his agents bills drawn on Portuguese merchants in Lisbon or Oporto, by firms in Hamburg, France, Amsterdam, and even Genoa and Leghorn. London is becoming an important exchange centre.

[1] *Cal. Treas. Books & Papers, 1735–8*, 314–15. This is not made clear by Shillington and Chapman, op. cit., p. 249.

If Braund's bills of exchange show the growing position
of London as a bill-market, his 'commission business' in
transhipping gold to the Amsterdam firm of bankers,
Clifford & Sons, limited though it was, stresses its development as a bullion market. From 1758 to 1761 he
shipped to them in men-of-war, either Dutch or English,
£3,831 3s. 11d. in five shipments. Since only one of them
was in silver, he was not taking part in the process whereby
gold was driving out silver from the English market. The
gold was exported in the form of foreign coins, and payment was made for them by bill of exchange from Amsterdam, after deduction of his commission, freight, brokerage,
and postage, all of which Braund charged to the account
of Jackson, Branfill, and Goddard. It was a very minor part
of his activities, and the sums handled were small, but it
has value as an illustration of the working of a notable and
growing English commerce.

By the end of 1761, however, though the price of gold
had reached its height, and the exchange was only slightly
higher than the year before, both the shipments of gold
and the number of bills of exchange entered, began to fall
off slightly. It is possible that the negotiations for peace
and the anxiety which existed for it in England began to
suggest a cautious hesitance as to the continued rise in the
price of gold. After the peak price in 1761, indeed, it fell
fairly steadily, and throughout 1762 did not again reach £4.
Still more important to Braund were conditions in Portugal
itself. By the later part of 1761 it was clearly about to
become concerned in the Seven Years War and was in
danger of invasion by Spain. By December 1761, when the
English ambassador left Madrid, a rupture was certain, and
although the invasion which followed was finally defeated
by English forces, the position was not reassuring for
merchants during the early months of the year. There
was an abrupt fall in the rate of the exchange between
13 November and 4 February from 5s. 6½d. to 5s. 5d.
Then, when by June the position seemed more secure, the
needs of a British Army in Portugal had brought the exchange rate up to the unusually high level of 5s. 7d.
Braund's activities, a little checked by the dangers of the

first part of the year, were finally stopped by the rise of exchange in the latter part. The import of bullion had temporarily ceased to be a profitable enterprise. No bills of exchange were sent from England after 6 April, and the imports of gold came to an abrupt end on 28 June. It is significant that about the same time a few of the remittances in payment of the old debts were sent, in the old way once again, in bills of exchange from Lisbon. Thus in the middle of 1762 his bullion trade ends as abruptly as the woollen trade had before, except for a single shipment in September 1763,[1] which seems to have been made to seize the chance of a transitory rise in the price of gold during the speculative fluctuations of that year of European post-war credit inflation.

There can be little doubt that it was the political circumstances of Europe which caused the trade to end when it did, just as they had encouraged its growth; for save for this 'commission business' the only active relations which still continued between the two firms were those necessary in the winding up of their business connexions. By the end of 1763, when the bullion trade ceased, Braund's accounts with them finally closed, and their name never again occurs in his books. In spite, however, of the shock which their prosperity had received in 1755 and the fact that Braund had lost heavily over them, Jackson, Branfill, and Goddard did not go bankrupt. Benjamin Branfill remained connected with the firm until his death, and Goddard was his executor. Branfill seems to have been still in Lisbon in partnership in 1765, but by 1767 had returned to London and set up as a Lisbon merchant to run the English side of their business in the same office as his uncle. Here he began a successful business career, the firm of Branfill and Goddard was recognized as Lisbon correspondent of the East India Company, and Branfill himself rose to the position of

---

[1] There is a reference in the *Gentleman's Magazine* of May 1763 to the new rise in the price of bullion, which continued with fluctuations for some months; p. 256, '. . . The demand for gold in coin is so great, that the Jews now give 4 guineas an ounce, so that we may soon expect to have that as scarce as silver. The reason is, the Dutch are drawing their money from our funds, in order to accommodate the French, who give 8 per cent.'

Director of the Bank of England and Manager of the Sun Fire Office.[1]

With the closing of his accounts with Jackson, Branfill, and Goddard, William Braund severed for ever a connexion with the Portuguese trade that had lasted for over twenty years, but when he had dropped his connexions in the woollen trade he had already half-changed. From pure dealing in bullion to pure finance as a specialized underwriter was a small step; and with the conclusion of the Portuguese trade Braund left the ranks of the merchant to swell those of the pure financier. A representative merchant, he was also to be a representative financier, for just as the years of his activities as a woollens and bullion merchant were those of general activity, so the years of his growing underwriting business were formative in the rise of Lloyd's.

The change, moreover, was a shrewd one in the circumstances of the time, as the course of the Portuguese trade of the next half-century was to show, for the great days of the Portugal trade were definitely passing away.

---

[1] India Office. E. I. Co., Ct. Bk. 79, f. 413, 18 Mar. 1771. The firm had sometimes done business for the East India Company as early as 1747. See ibid., *Miscellaneous Home Letters received*, vol. 35, No. 126a, letter of 11 Nov. 1749.

EXPORT OF WOOLLENS. 1753.

Date of Shipping.	Goods in Bales.	Numbers.	Date of Net Price.	First Cost and Charges. £ s. d.	Net Price. £ s. d.	Profit. £ s. d.
Feb. 12	6 ord. long ells.	405–10	Mar. 21, 1754	286 18 0	300 19 0	14 1 0
Mar. 27	12 long bays.	413–24	July 7 } June 2 } 1753	903 6 4	933 7 0	30 0 8
Mar. 27	9 long bays.	426–34	June 22 } July 7, 1753	665 7 6	733 0 0	67 12 6
Mar. 27	2 long bays.	435–6	July 7, 1753	172 14 6	190 0 0	17 5 6
Apr. 2	2 durants.	437–8	Mar. 25, 1754	182 0 0	209 0 0	27 0 0
Apr. 2	4 shalloons.	439–42	Mar. 25, 1754	359 9 10	372 4 0	12 14 2
May 10	11 long bays.	443–53	July 7 } Nov. 14 } 1753	573 5 10	672 10 0	99 4 2
June 8	1 scarlet cloth.	454	April 8, 1754	111 11 0	109 6 0	Loss, 2 5 0
July 7	1 durants.	455	Dec. 31, 1754	80 3 0	94 0 0	13 17 0
*Aug. 15	5 blankets.	(see note)	. . .	(151 1 0)	—	
Aug. 28	4 long bays.	460–3	Nov. 14, 1753	172 16 0	198 4 0	25 8 8
Aug. 28	2 durants.	464–5	Nov. 24, 1753	175 5 9	201 10 0	26 4 3
Aug. 28	1 shalloons.	466	Nov. 24, 1753	83 17 0	84 11 0	14 0
Oct. 31	1 scarlet cloth.	467	April 8, 1754	111 11 0	131 3 0	19 12 0
Oct. 31	1 blue cloth.	468	April 8, 1754	86 13 0	92 10 0	5 17 0
Oct. 31	1 shalloons.	469	Dec. 31, 1754	87 19 0	91 0 0	3 0 8
Dec. 13	15 long bays.	470–84	April 8, 1754	956 16 4	1,109 13 0	152 16 8
Dec. 13	2 Colchester bays.	485–6	April 8, 1754	117 2 8	127 0 0	9 17 4
Dec. 13	6 long bays.	487–92	April 8, 1754	335 16 7	374 18 0	39 1 5
Total	86 bales.			£5,462 13 8	£6,024 15 0	£564 6 4

Average Profit : Approximately 10½.

* For this consignment of blankets, Philip Jackson of London paid cash on 31 Aug. 1753, together with 5s. commission. It was therefore bought and shipped, it is to be presumed, either on his behalf or on that of Jackson, Branfill, and Goddard themselves, for whom he may have been acting.

III

MARINE INSURANCE IN THE MID-EIGHTEENTH CENTURY

NO one aspect of the development of commercial as distinct from industrial aggregation which marked the eighteenth century, is more important than that in the sphere of marine insurance, which was preparing the way for the autonomous organization of Lloyd's. It is an aspect on which, however, our information is very incomplete. What certain knowledge we have of this period of the growth of marine insurance comes primarily from the two parliamentary inquiries of 1718–20[1] and of 1810,[2] in the evidence of both of which there is much useful detail; between these there is little but the contemporary treatises on insurance, the debates and acts of parliament, and the Law Reports. William Braund's career as an underwriter is, therefore, important, for it covers the years when information is slightest, and the time which made possible and necessary the organization which finally emerged. Even before 1741, the year in which his extant accounts begin, until his death in 1774, he was occupied in underwriting, at first as a minor, at last as almost his sole activity. It was an important time, and Braund's increasing specialization in insurance is in itself significant. It was the age which established the dominance in England of the individual underwriter, grouped in the unique institution of Lloyd's, in the place of the joint stock insurance company which was growing up elsewhere. By 1741 the individual underwriters had easily surmounted the dangers of the competition set up in 1720 when the two 'bubble' monopoly insurance companies were founded: the Royal Exchange Assurance Corporation and the London Assurance Corporation. They were indeed gaining from the prohibition of all other joint stock enterprise, and of partnership in

[1] Brit. Mus. (N. R.), 357 b, 3/30. *The Special Report from the Committee Appointed to Inquire into and Examine the several Subscriptions for Fisheries, Insurances . . . &c., London, 1720.*

[2] *Accounts and Papers, Reports, &c., 1810, iv, on Marine Insurance.*

marine insurance, which the companies' statutory monopoly entailed. At the same time English trade and shipping were expanding steadily, and, most important of all, England was in the midst of the series of commercial and maritime wars (Braund's activities cover two of them) which were to lead marine insurance to its full organization in the early years of the next century. In 1676 Molloy had thought it difficult to insure a 'trading voyage' at all, for 'this Policy being general and dangerous, seldom procures Subscriptions, or at least very chargeable ones'.[1] In 1752 a prominent underwriter and the richest of the West Indian merchants agreed on the difficulties in the way of effecting insurances at all times to Jamaica,[2] while it was still the mark of the great merchant to save by not insuring at all.[3] By 1810 it was the boast of John Angerstein,[4] the first great name in English insurance, in the midst of a European war, that 'every Insurance almost can be done with fair connections, and at a considerable advance of Premium' among the underwriters at Lloyd's.

William Braund's accounts bearing on the subject are found in the following books:

1. His *Journals*. There are three journals of Braund's; the rough journal, 1741–4 and after a gap 1750–64, and the two volumes of the fair journal, 1758–74. Into the rough journal until its break, and in its turn into the fair journal, there are copied every month the sums paid to insurance-brokers, or deducted by them from balance in hand, for losses, averages, and other payments. The fair journal also adds to these entries the premiums owed to Braund by the brokers. In the rough journal, however, after its resumption in 1750 no insurance entries are made, the journal being now kept entirely for trade. Insurance entries were presumably henceforth made directly from the separate rough insurance journal which Postlethwayt

---

[1] C. Molloy, *De Jure Maritimo et Navali*, 1676, p. 253.

[2] *Parliamentary History*, xiv. 1213. Sir John Barnard and William Beckford.

[3] Beckford said in the debate referred to above that he seldom insured. Cf. *A Letter to a Member of Parliament*, By a Merchant. (*c.* 1720), p. 2 (Brit. Mus. (N. R.), 357 b, 3/62). It speaks of the 'Rich Merchants, who never make any Insurance at all, and can therefore afford to sell their Goods at a cheaper Rate'.

[4] 1810 Report, loc. cit., p. 64.

advised all insurers to keep,[1] into an earlier volume (unfortunately lost) of the fair journal which has come down to us. Thus information is, during the earlier years covered by the accounts, very incomplete; there is some in the rough journal 1741–4, none for the years 1744–7; then the cash book begins to give some help, and continues to be the only guide until the fair journal and the Ledger F begin in 1758. The fair journals then run through without a break until Braund's death, though in his later years, when his trading activities cease, the entries are confined to his insurance business, ships' dividends, and returns from shares and land.

2. The *Cash Book*. The cash book, 1747–74, the only authority on insurance business from 1747 until 1758, contains not only such minor entries as law charges, presents to the servants of brokers, and occasional averages, but also the sums paid in by the brokers in settlement of their accounts, a settlement usually made once a year.[2] It gives, thus, some indication of those with whom he was doing steady business from 1747 to 1758.

3. His *Ledgers*. Here he enters the accounts taken from the fair journal under the name of the various brokers and merchants with whom he deals, and also keeps a special Account of Insurances. In this he enters annually his estimated profit (there is never a loss) by the year's underwriting. These estimates cannot, however, by themselves be considered as a gauge to the extent and profit of his ventures, since, as Weskett remarks, ' The usual way with considerate insurers, when they write off profit upon insurance account, is to leave, besides the premiums not run off, a sum at guess sufficient to answer what demands remain unsettled '.[3] Since Braund was a cautious man, these sums varied greatly, not only with the extent of his commitments but also with the conditions of the time. During the years of war his reserve grew so greatly that for some time

---

[1] s.v. 'Mercantile Accountantship'.

[2] The usual time for the brokers to make their settlements was January to May. J. Weskett, *A Complete Digest of the Theory, Laws and Practice of Insurance*, 1781, p. 63, complains of their slowness in settling, which he alleges to have become more marked in the second half century.

[3] Weskett, op. cit., p. 295.

he scarcely transferred anything to the account of profit at all. The ledgers run in two volumes from 1758 until his death.

4. The *Journals of Risks*. These very important accounts run from 1759 to 1774 in two volumes. They consist of entries of the particulars of every risk undertaken, under the name of the broker or merchant for whom it was done. A typical entry is:

Mar. 7th 1759. £200. Grayhound, Turner, Smyrna Lond°.
    G. John Harding 7 gu. £14.[1]

These risks must have been copied in from the alphabet or risk book which each underwriter carried with him to Lloyd's, to keep a check on the 'slip' which the broker made out before preparing the policy.

These accounts, particularly the journals of risks, are valuable since they begin a good half-century earlier than any records of risks hitherto used,[2] and they are interesting in so far as they bring out the extent and flexibility of the insurance system as developed by the middle of the eighteenth century. They indicate in themselves how inevitable was a development both in law and organization to control the vigorous and complicated business which had grown up in marine insurance.

The nature of this two-fold development, law and organization, needs some elaboration; and indeed before investigating the insurance business of Braund it is necessary to

---

[1] i. e. £200 underwritten, ship *Grayhound*, Turner master, on voyage from Smyrna to London, on goods the property of John Harding at 7 guineas per cent. Premium £14 (1s. in each guinea was deducted for broker's commission).

[2] J. T. Danson, *Our Next War*, 1894, used the risk books of J. Janson for 1805–10 and 1815, of E. Allfrey for 1810, and of G. Hobson for 1811–16. (See p. 66 of his work.) The Janson accounts are now in the British Museum, Add. MSS. 34669–76.

Mr. W. R. Dawson, Honorary Librarian of Lloyd's, informs me that among a batch of old policies recently presented to Lloyd's is one signed by William Braund. Its particulars are:
Policy in the name of James Gordon.
London to Madeira.
St. Francesco de Paula ; Master, Manoel Fernandez.
    £300 on goods at 2¼ guineas per cent.
                Signed £100 W. G. Freeman.
                       £100 William Braund.
                       £100 Richard Gililant.
Dated 19 May 1761.

examine at some length the contemporary position of insurance from various points of view. The eighteenth century saw at first more clearly the development in the law than that which was to come in the organization of insurance. The legal development of insurance was an important part of the great reception of merchant custom into English law. The advance in insurance practice in the courts during these years was both rapid and far reaching. Park, in his *System of the Law of Marine Insurances*,[1] has guessed, and Martin, in his *History of Lloyd's*,[2] has repeated as a fact, in illustration of the backwardness of insurance law when Mansfield set his hand to it, that only sixty cases had been reported in the Common Law courts up to that time (1756). The estimate seems accurate, but when it is considered how few of the cases are reported before the later years of the seventeenth century, it is less remarkable that during the following years there should have been so few than that there should have been so many. Contemporaries certainly, well before Mansfield's activities began, considered themselves to be in the midst of a period of rapidly developing insurance law. Beawes remarked in 1752 that they had seen lately 'the most famous Trials that ever employed our Courts on this Subject'.[3] An undue importance given to the statements of Park, made in his desire to extol Mansfield, has indeed tended to hide from later writers on insurance the conditions which made possible Mansfield's undoubtedly epoch-making work on insurance law. It was only because there were already a number, and, as the complexities of insurance grew, an increasing number of insurance cases before the courts, that Mansfield was able to pursue his policy of obtaining on each important point that arose a special case, on which he could make an authoritative statement in full court. It was only because his predecessors had not been leaving cases altogether to the jury that he was able, carrying his colleagues on the bench with him, to create that amalgam of precedent and innovation which

---

[1] J. A. Park, 1787, p. xl. The most noted eighteenth-century work on insurance written in England.

[2] F. Martin, *The History of Lloyd's and of Marine Insurance in Great Britain*, 1876, p. 121.

[3] W. Beawes, op cit., p. 264.

could be embodied in the Common Law. It was only because there was wide interest and knowledge, wider in merchant cases than in others (where the complexities of law had by that time defeated the plain man's understanding), that he could obtain at the Guildhall the intelligent merchant juries which were his pride.[1] The books for the instruction of merchants are an illustration of the interest in understanding insurance cases; Braund's accounts are an illustration of the extent to which insurers had recourse to law. Between February 1742 and April 1751 there are no fewer than eight references in his cash book to lawyers' costs in insurance disputes. Even Mansfield's insistence on the consolidation of insurance cases, so that each underwriter should not (as under Common Law he could) claim to be sued separately, was important rather as a check on the abuses of unscrupulous underwriters than as an innovation affecting insurance in general. This convention had been in force for years[2]; the cases in which William Braund was concerned were invariably thus consolidated.

For, just as the 'opinion of the Bourse' had given a validity to the usages of the bill of exchange as strong or stronger than those of law, the Bourse being, though unorganized, a unit, and credit on the Bourse a condition of survival; so though no organization existed, the opinion of the coffee-houses, in particular, of course, of Lloyd's Coffee-house, controlled the underwriters of London. For just as on the Bourse, when the growth of business made difficult the personal knowledge on which such credit must depend, there grew up the class of intermediaries, dealers in foreign exchange, bankers, and bill-brokers, who kept together the unwieldy mass of merchants; so the creation of the unity of London's insurance market in the eighteenth century rested primarily with the increasingly important class of insurance broker. It was not till well into the nineteenth century that a curious fact became evident. Unlike the bill-broker, who was rising to an increasingly dominant position in the organization of the money market

---

[1] Campbell, *Lives of the Chief Justices*, vol. ii, p. 443.
[2] This had been pointed out during the course of the investigations of 1718–20. *The Special Report . . .*, op. cit., The Attorney-General's Report, 1719, p. 43.

(for indeed the great power of the bill-broker dates almost entirely from the nineteenth century), the insurance-broker was losing his control of the insurance market in favour of that elaborately developed control by the body of under-writers themselves, which is known as Lloyd's to-day.

The reverse side of the development of law was, there-fore, the growth, not indeed of the organization of insurance, but of aggregation preparing the way for it. It was the distinction between these two divergent but complementary aspects of progress, law and organization, that Magens and Weskett tried to stress when they urged the devolution of certain types of insurance cases, but certain types alone, to merchants' courts.[1] They were asking, in fact, from a merchant tribunal the kind of control which the nine-teenth-century organization of Lloyd's was to give them.

In England it seems now clear that Marine Insurance was introduced by the Italian merchants, for long probably exercised among themselves alone, for though Giovanni da Uzzano mentions insurance between London and Pisa in 1442,[2] it appears entirely unknown in the fifteenth-cen-tury staple trade. In the sixteenth century, however, it came into fairly general use among merchants, though not sufficiently to obscure the reputation of the Venetians as the greatest insurers of Europe.[3] Despite the boasts of the Insurance Act of 1601,[4] England was not during the six-teenth century a great insurance mart, as was either Ant-werp or Venice. In 1581 the Spanish representative at London told the King of Spain of the efforts of a Genoese to insure gold, silver, jewels, and other merchandise on two ships from Terceira to ports in Brittany or England. ' Some merchants here have already underwritten £2,000 of it at 8 per cent. premium, on condition that if these ships should be seized by your Majesty's fleet they are not

---

[1] N. Magens, *A Tract on Insurances*, 1755, p. 428 ; Weskett, op. cit., p. 180.

[2] *Pratica della Mercatura*, 1442, printed by Pagnini ; *Della Decima . . . della Moneta e della Mercatura*, 1765, ii. 119 ; W. W. Blackstock, *The Historical Literature of Sea and Fire Insurance in Great Britain 1547–1810*, Manchester, 1910. A useful bibliography.

[3] *Cal. Venetian State Papers*, 1603, p. 91, No. 128.

[4] 43 Elizabeth, c. 12.

to pay. As this is not a great business centre they will not get much more underwritten here.'[1]

In the seventeenth century it grew, however, amazingly. The sixteenth-century attempt to found an official registry for policies was not a success; it only meant that private and public policies flourished side by side, and by the eighteenth century only the terms private and public offices survived, the latter being applied to the new joint stock companies set up in 1720. Still less successful than this very partial attempt at organization were the demands made in the later seventeenth century for patents for the control of insurance by a joint stock company, for though it was declared in 1662 by applicants that, if they were given their chance the London offices would become 'the insurance office for Europe',[2] no serious attempt was made to found such an enterprise. Under these conditions the private underwriter remained throughout its history the moulding force of English insurance, and in the eighteenth century the very measure, the founding of the two joint stock companies, which seemed about to destroy him, served by restricting the formation of others to protect the individual against company competition. Moreover, by forbidding partnership dealings it served eventually to bring to the fore the man whose chief occupation was not that of a merchant but of a specialized underwriter.

The later seventeenth century itself seems to have seen little specialization of insurance, and no insurance centre but the Royal Exchange. Nevertheless, the growth of its elaboration, and the increase of the speculative element in it (it was said in the law courts of the eighteenth century that insurances 'interest or no interest', mere wager policies, and with them the reinsurance of risks for speculative reasons, grew up after the Revolution),[3] meant that a

---

[1] *Cal. Spanish State Papers, 1581*, p. 158, No. 121. Bernardino de Mendoza to the King of Spain.

[2] *Cal. State Papers, Domestic, 1662*, p. 615, No. 53. C. Wright and C. E. Fayle, *A History of Lloyd's*, p. 40, who refer to this proposal (following Blackstock they wrongly attributed it to 1660), have missed that of 1673 by Col. Dymock and others to the same effect (*Cal. State Pap. Dom., 1673*, p. 76).

[3] *Depaba [Da Paiba] v. Ludlow*, Comyns 361, 1720 C. B. English Reports, 92, p. 1112.

definite insurance interest was in existence. The range of risks taken was still indeed limited, but the number was increasing, and the methods of settling premiums,[1] average and return of premiums, were those of a big market. Malynes, who wrote the first English observations on insurance in 1622, and Molloy following him fifty-four years later, looked with suspicion on insurance effected on the ship itself, the premium on which was estimated to be almost double that on goods, as 'much subject to Averidges and other casualties, especially if it be upon a Shippe that cannot drinke of all waters, whereunto divers men may lay claime'.[2] Cross risks (voyages between two foreign ports) when at any distance he urges the underwriter not to undertake at all, and insurance to places where trade is prohibited, such as Guinea and the West Indies, should be undertaken only under very high premiums indeed. Molloy's comment on the difficulty of insuring trading voyages has already been quoted.[3]

In spite of these limitations, however, England was, by the beginning of the eighteenth century, competing with Amsterdam as the chief insuring centre of the world, on account, it was usually said, of the cheap money in those two centres.[4] Before 1755, when Magens wrote, it was generally agreed that England had won the dominant position,[5] a position which she was never to lose. From early in the century much foreign business was carried out in London (just as was foreign investment in English stocks) through English merchants for foreign correspondents. This was done in several ways. Before the prohibition of reinsurance of risks in 1746[6] the agents of English

---

[1] The distinction between summer and winter risks, and the relation between them, was already fixed by custom. Malynes, op. cit., p. 159, advised an increase of 2 per cent. on the premium in winter, and of 1 per cent. when 'an East or North-east winde driveth from the land for Spaine'.

[2] Malynes, op. cit., p. 148.   [3] p. 43, above.

[4] There were of course other Continental centres of insurance, e.g. Rouen, the importance of which is brought out by an interesting document recently edited by Mr. W. R. Dawson, under the title of *Marine Underwriting at Rouen 1727-42*.

[5] N. Magens, *Tract on Insurances*. He is particularly interesting in this connexion on account of his insurance experience in Hamburg, where, indeed, this work in a shorter form was first published.

[6] By 19 Geo. II, c. 37. The act was intended to check wagering.

merchants in foreign ports used often to insure the ships and goods of foreigners abroad, their principal then re-insuring the risk in England. Sometimes, as in the case of Sir John Barnard, who had his agent at Cadiz, they made thereby a gain of 100 per cent. on the different levels of premiums on the bigger and smaller markets.[1] This indi-rect insurance of foreign risks on the English market was, however, never of great importance; the chief method used was direct insurance in London by the English merchant on behalf of his foreign correspondent, and an arrange-ment whereby the English merchant guaranteed, for a small extra charge, the insurances which they had effected. This method remained general until, by 1810, confidence in the solidity of the London underwriters had led a con-siderable proportion of the foreign insurers to forego the guarantee altogether.[2]

This development was almost entirely one of the eigh-teenth century. While it was taking place, moreover, the English market was extending in another way. Provincial centres were also growing up, of which Bristol was the chief, and they enlarged the London market by carrying on their business in relation to it, sometimes, indeed, it must be admitted with fraudulent intent. Unusual or large risks were almost always transferred from them to London, and, on the other hand, an abnormally large risk in London often found underwriters both there and in the provincial centres. When in 1747 £105,800 was insured on the Spanish prize, the *Nympha*, from Lisbon to London,[3] a risk of most unusual magnitude at that time, it was under-written at London, Bristol, and Exeter.

With the increase of trade, there was also an increase in the variety of risks. Their numbers grew, and the develop-ment in insurance on cross risks and trading voyages was very great. There was a development of the time risk, with special consideration of the needs of packet boats and of the privateers (a subject in themselves) who might cruise the sea-routes for many months in time of war.[4] Insurances

---

[1] *The Special Report* of 1720, op. cit., Attorney-General's Report, 1719, p. 44; cf. N. Magens, op. cit., p. 95.   [2] Report of 1810, *passim*.
[3] N. Magens, op. cit., p. 222.   [4] Weskett, op. cit., s.v. 'Privateers', p. 412 seq.

on lives, long known, became more common, though they were often most undesirable wager policies,[1] and insurance against fire and other dangers in foreign lands was often negotiated. William Braund, for instance, regularly underwrote an insurance for 2 per cent. per annum on a sugar factory belonging to an English merchant, Charles Dingley, at St. Petersburg. Ordinary marine risks had become, by a process of custom occasionally assisted by law,[2] divided into various categories; viz. those on: Ship (S), Goods (G), Money (Mo) (gold and silver, distinct from other merchandise because of the special conditions of their trade), Bottomry Bonds (B), and Respondentia Bonds (Ra).[3] Except where occasionally he underwrites a risk of a special character, such as a cargo of paper money from Quebec after the acquisition of Canada by England, Braund has in his books against each entry the appropriate symbol. It is interesting to note that this must be the customary background of the S, G, and SG of Lloyd's early printed policies, which for long puzzled expounders, and may even now be not fully explained.[4]

These developments demanded a great increase in the specialized knowledge of the underwriter, for marine insurance has always required as much consideration of the particular as the general. Not only were adjustments of premium necessary for winter and summer risks, but every voyage required its special conditions. The consolidation of these into custom was itself an illustration of the great growth of the solidarity and strength of the market. Privateers, a very common form of time risk during war, were habitually insured free of all average;[5] a packet boat, as

---

[1] A singularly scandalous illustration of this was an insurance wager on the lives of their fathers by two heirs. *Earl of March* v. *Pigot*, 5 Burr. 2802, 1771, B. R. English Reports, 98, pp. 471–2.

[2] As in the case of respondentia and bottomry. *Glover* v. *Black*, 3 Burr. 1394, Trin. Term. 3 Geo. III B. R. Mansfield said that since respondentia and bottomry were 'a particular species of Insurance in themselves' intelligent persons always specify it in their policies.

[3] There occur occasionally in the Braund papers two other classifications, ff. [freight ?] and I. I have not discovered what they stand for.

[4] Wright and Fayle, op. cit., pp. 132–5.

[5] *Da Costa* v. *Firth*, 4 Burr. 1966, 1766, B. R. English Reports, 98, pp. 24–5.

King's property, neither paid nor received average.[1] The East India Company had in their charter-parties special conditions with regard to average, which were by 1765 recognized as customary in the courts of law.[2] Ships, from Greenland or the Baltic were often declared in the policy free of all average under 5 per cent. from ice.[3] In the hurricane season West Indian premiums almost doubled, and during war the condition 'with convoy' would often halve the premium. Most significant of all, the addition of the general memorandum to policies in 1749 represents not only the results of custom but their deliberate adoption by the market as a rule. All these and many other points had constantly to be kept in mind, so that the policy which reflected them had, in the eighteenth century, become so complicated that writers declared that all past problems discussed with regard to it had ceased to be applicable.[4]

It has been argued by some that it was this complexity which led directly to the need for the specialized underwriter, for they alone could handle such intricate matters. This argument appears, however, to be incorrect. The specialized underwriter grew up out of the expansion of business, like all specialized finance interests, and played an important part on the market ; but, as long as the organization for procuring information was scanty and ill-arranged, the advantage continued to lie with the merchant, who had in certain directions his own information. Even in 1810 it was to the merchants with their specialized knowledge of the conditions of one branch of trade, that John Julius Angerstein went to find the leaders to write the first line of his policies, and set the terms which the other underwriters would follow.[5] The specialized underwriter became prominent in the insurance market only about the middle of the eighteenth century, just at the time when other financial specialists were rising, and when Braund himself was becoming one. Big dealers or small, and there is no reason to think that the scale of their business was in any way

---

[1] Weskett, op. cit., s.v. 'General Average', p. 257.
[2] *Heaton* v. *Rucker*, 3 Burr. 1707, 1765, B. R. English Reports, 97, pp. 1057–61.
[3] *Gardiner* v. *Croasdale*, 2 Burr. 904, 1760, B.R. English Reports, 97, pp. 625–6.
[4] W. Beawes, op. cit., p. 264.
[5] 1810 Report, p. 60.

above the average, they became in time the men who could
be found at Lloyd's at all seasons, and they learned to mix
their risks so that 'the partiality of keeping to particular
trades is less at Lloyd's than at any other place'.[1] Important as such a body must be, however, they were for the
time swamped by the larger body of merchant underwriters, who both insured their own risks and underwrote
those of others.

All this growth in extent and complexity of business,
without any corresponding growth in organization, was
made possible only by the closest personal relationship,
which was promoted by the use of Lloyd's Coffee-house as
the centre of insurance activities. It was a custom which
does not appear to have grown up until 1720, and it never became altogether general until the days when Lloyd's ceased
to be a coffee-house and became an organization. From
1750 at the latest, however, its predominance in the London
insurance market was overwhelming, and it had become
the means of a certain degree of common policy, and even
(though only indirectly) of organization. The adoption of
the Memorandum to the printed policy in 1749, for instance, seems certainly to have been the result of some
agreement at Lloyd's.[2] In the same way the formation of
the society which controlled Lloyd's Register of Shipping,[3]
to which most of the prominent men of the coffee-house
belonged, was the direct result of the importance of the
coffee-house as a centre. It seems probable that, like those
who attended Jonathan's, the stock-jobbing coffee-house, its
habitués made an early and abortive attempt at the organization they only later achieved. In 1757 John Eliot, a
quaker merchant beginning his career as an insurer, writes
that he went to Lloyd's and 'subscribed the book at 2 guineas
a year'.[4] In the coffee-house in Lombard Street the underwriters sat in their boxes, each in his known place, where
the brokers continually going to and fro could find those

---

[1] John Julius Angerstein, evidence before the 1810 Committee, op. cit.,
p. 67.

[2] See Wright and Fayle, op. cit., pp. 143–5.

[3] *Annals of Lloyd's Register*, 1884.

[4] *Eliot Papers*, compiled by E. Howard, 1893, i. 31. My attention was drawn
to this entry by Mr. Warren Dawson.

with whom they did business. Shipping information of ever growing variety and importance was posted up when it came in by the master or the waiters acting for him. Even Lloyd's great new building of to-day shows in its general plan traces of the coffee-house, its remote proto-type.

In such an assembly leadership was essential, and this need was the more marked on account of the new elements which the expansion of the market was bringing in. It was said at the time that the insurance business of Amsterdam began to decline when the number of underwriters began to grow under the stimulus of war-time profits.[1] This was certainly not true of London. As each succeeding war brought in the new underwriters, under conditions where skill and experience were at a discount; when considerations of average, usually predominant when settling a premium, were entirely subordinate, the business of marine underwriting began to contain certainly some very rotten elements. At the same time it gained the elements of enter-prise which, under proper control, were as much the conditions of its development as was the real financial stability and uprightness which observers feared it might lose. The control came partly through the growth of leading underwriters, but far more, as has already been indicated, through the brokers. It is the development of the position of the broker, personal and functional, in the London market, which must be watched.

By the second half of the eighteenth century the position of the insurance-broker was far more developed than that of the contemporary bill-broker, inasmuch as the former fulfilled wider functions and included among them that of a kind of guarantee which lifted him out of the ranks of the pure intermediaries. This aspect of the bill-brokers' duties was not fully developed[2] by 1810, while the insurance-broker's growth had already reached and even passed its zenith. The position of the insurance-brokers as guarantors grew from the fact that they became the central point of a development of credit. They received the premiums

---

[1] W. Beawes, op. cit., p. 289.
[2] J. H. Clapham, *An Economic History of Modern Britain*, pp. 260–2.

from the merchants insuring, and were responsible for passing them on to the underwriters. Since they also received
payments for losses, averages, or return of premium from
the underwriters it became common for them to retain
these sums in the case of the underwriters with whom they
did steady business, making annual settlements with them.
By this arrangement they then were able to give considerable credit facilities to merchants in the payment of premiums, and in doing so were at the same time guarantors
to the underwriters for the premiums due to them from the
insurers, and were responsible (in fact though not in law)
to the insurers for the soundness of the underwriters. Near
the end of the century, at least, a further custom arose, by
analogy with that of English merchants when they insured
for correspondents abroad, for the broker to take an extra
percentage payment, and add a legal to his non-legal responsibility for the underwriters.[1] This extra burden, however, developing at a time when the needs of the market
were already outstripping the capacities of the brokers'
control, never became universal.

It was this strategic position which the brokers enjoyed
that gave them their functional importance in the organization of marine insurance. The merchant who wished to
insure, unguarded by any organization guaranteeing the
security of his underwriters, was forced to reply upon the
judgement of his broker, unless he himself played a part at
Lloyd's. The underwriters, who were many, growing in
numbers, often newcomers, and on the whole small men,
sought to obtain the business which the broker had to offer.
Under such conditions the brokers' position was bound to
be dominant. Weskett,[2] writing in 1781, with the bitterness

---

[1] Evidence for 1810 Report, op. cit., p. 114. Evidence of John Rogers,
broker.

[2] Weskett's *Treatise* is a work of learning which has been unduly neglected.
His introduction shows him also, however, as a disappointed underwriter, hostile
to the whole system of insurance. All that can be gathered about the underwriting experiences that so embittered him is that he was involved in several
insurance disputes. (See op. cit., pp. 264–5 and 518–19, s.v. 'Greenland' and 'Ship
or Ships', and *Ratcliffe and Bostock* v. *Weskett*, p. 233 seq., s.v. 'Fraud'.) He is
described in Baldwin's Directory of 1783 as a merchant of Jeffery's Square, St.
Mary Ax. In 1782 he published a *Plan of the Chamber of Commerce*, (*in the
Building late the King's Arms Tavern, Cornhill*) *or Office, for Consultation, opinion*

of an intransigent underwriter, complains of their arrogance and fraud, their pressure on the unorganized underwriter. It is of course a partial and exaggerated picture, but it was true to the extent that the broker of credit could always have the upper hand. It was he who had to judge the reliability of any underwriter whom he allowed on his books, and a broker of good connexion would exclude rigidly any underwriter of whose security there could be the least doubt, or who was known for litigiousness in the settlement of claims. Once on a broker's books the underwriter had to take the bad risks with the good. In the absence of the average adjusters of the nineteenth century the broker was relied on greatly for the settlement of claims; even after the development of Lloyd's Register underwriters waived, in the case of their regular brokers, the difference of ships' class ; and many maintained that during the dangerous autumn months of premium adjustment, underwriters who were not anxious to write the more fluctuating risks found it easier to avoid the coffee-house altogether than to alienate the brokers with whom they dealt. When it is added that the brokers tended to work in groups, giving part of their commissions to each other,[1] one can see how strong their position was in a limited market kept together by personal connexion.

This functional importance was, moreover, accompanied by considerable personal importance. The broker was in most cases also an underwriter, and, in the days when the specialized underwriter was only rising, formed a very prominent part of that class. Weskett complained that often policies could be seen on which there were more names of brokers than of underwriters and merchants.[2] John Julius Angerstein was only the greatest of a number of brokers who were also underwriters. The great underwriter of the

---

and Advice, Information and Assistance, In all Commercial, Insurance and Maritime Affairs and Matters of Trade in general (Guildhall Tracts, 329 (4)). He announces that in default of the merchant courts, &c., found abroad, he offers this substitute under a skilled ' conductor', who has ' for many years given extraordinary and peculiar attention to insurance '. The tract is anonymous, but it refers to Weskett's work, which is also advertised at the end.

[1] 1810 Report, *passim.*
[2] Weskett, op. cit., p. 65.

Napoleonic Wars was, it would seem, the creation almost entirely of the years of war inflation and wealth, though the scale of dealings had before been steadily rising. In 1720 it might have been true to say that more than £100 to £200 was rarely written on a line; by the time of the French Revolution this is no longer so. Nevertheless the day of huge lines had not yet come. In 1755 Magens quoted £500 and £1,000 as big lines.[1] Braund only once exceeded the latter on his own account, writing in 1762 £2,000 on bullion on a man-of-war, and though lines of £500 are fairly common in his books, his average is about £150. It was the rise of the great specialist underwriter that quietly eclipsed the personal power of the broker, and his rise was assisted by the development of agency and of the syndicate of underwriters. Not only was the great underwriter not yet found in the eighteenth century, but what small beginnings of agency there were, were apt to centre in the brokers themselves, who quite often seem to have acted as agents for others, as the firm of Moffatts may have done for Braund in his last years.[2] It is interesting in this connexion to notice that the Braund papers show that brokers had already begun the practice, which continued into the present century, of 'running an office account'. In 1720 brokers had been accused of, and had denied vigorously, the use of fictitious names whereby they underwrote their own policies.[3] Braund's papers show that it was common for brokers in the second half of the century to arrange that underwriters should write on their behalf on their own policies. Braund wrote in this way for four firms of brokers for many years, generally on their own policies, but sometimes on those of others. The sums involved were usually small, and it is clear that the broker considered it as a simple means of supplementing his brokerage.

The whole insurance interest, bound together by the

---

[1] N. Magens, op. cit., p. 222.

[2] Andrew Moffatt appears, from the early policies now possessed by Lloyd's, to have been acting as agent in the years from 1764 to 1766 for W. G. Freeman and Thos. Corbett.

[3] *The Office Keeper's Answer to a Scandalous Reflection on them.* . . . (c. 1720), Brit. Mus. (N. R.), 357 b, 30/73.

insurance-broker through his personal position and his function on the market, was a special interest in the City, but not at all cut off from other interests. In the same way the underwriter was seldom, even when specialized in the sense of not being a merchant, confined altogether to the insurance market, and the brokers, themselves specialists of recent growth, never quite left their earlier activities. Some even maintained certain interests as merchants, or at least some connexion with a merchant firm ; some were ship-brokers and stock-brokers, and they tended, both in their connexion at Lloyd's and their spheres of action, to maintain contact with interests outside the insurance market. Charles Child and Nathaniel Fletcher were both part-owners of one of the East Indiamen in which William Braund had a share, and of which his brother Samuel was ship's husband. Samuel Bonham had a relative, Captain Pincent Bonham, prominent in the East India shipping interest. Andrew Moffatt was connected with the East India Company shipping, and with the merchant firm of J. Moffatt & Co. in the North America trade.[1] Though brokers rarely confined themselves to one class of risks, they nearly all had a connexion in which some special branch of insurance predominated. Eastland and Lewis handled chiefly Baltic trade risks ; Godin, Guion & Co., Continental risks, and the Jew brokers, Jewish risks to the West Indies or Mediterranean or elsewhere. The connexion of the brokers with certain branches of trade and shipping was, moreover, often made closer by their position as capitalists. The brokers, principally on account of the sums they were apt to have in hand on behalf of underwriters, appear to have taken a considerable part in supplying credit to members of that loosely defined entity, the London shipping interest. East Indiamen, when on voyage, drew on some of them, such as Andrew Moffatt, by draught or bill of exchange, for their expenses,[2] and it is striking how many of the loans on bottomry or respondentia insured in these accounts were made by the insurance brokers at Lloyd's.

[1] For these broker firms see Appendix IV.
[2] This is shown in the shipping papers of Samuel Braund.

This class of brokers, so important in its time, can be seen in the commercial directories emerging into strength from all manner of other pursuits. In the commercial organization of eighteenth-century London, the early years of a new financial phase had brought everywhere to the fore the financial intermediary: stock-brokers, bill-brokers, and a host of others, and unfriendly contemporaries looked appalled at the forms ' more savage than their Bulls and Bears' that flourished or swarmed obscurely in the City. Among them was, inevitably, a wide fringe of disreputability, and the men who composed it when they turned to the insurance market set afoot the most extraordinary gambling policies. It is of such men that Thomas Mortimer wrote in his indictment *Every Man his own Broker*.[1] But though in the mid-century even the most respectable underwriter might sometimes write such a policy (as Braund occasionally did) and though, moreover, a broker with the best business connexions would sometimes accept it, these elements did not stand for the most important part of the new broker interest at Lloyd's. The rapidity of their rise is shown by a comparison with 1720. Then only eleven names are found to sign a protest by the regular insurance-brokers, or ' office-keepers', about the Royal Exchange against attacks upon their business morality, and the broker is described in a contemporary broadsheet as a ' poor indigent Fellow who may be strongly tempted to impose upon me'.[2] Already, however, the regular brokers showed how the new elements were entering the business, for they spoke of a man who ' was not an Officer-Keeper, but one who acted as a broker for discounting Notes and did sometimes make Policies ',[3] and for whose conduct they did not hold themselves responsible. By 1741 Braund, as yet no more than a merchant who also underwrote a little, has on his books twenty-two brokers, of whom only two have any apparent connexion with the eleven broker firms of 1720; many of

[1] First edition in 1761.
[2] *A Second letter to a Member of Parliament*, by a Merchant (*c.* 1720). Brit. Mus. (N.R.), 357 b, 3/63.
[3] *The Office Keepers' Answer to a Scandalous Reflection on them* . . . (*c.* 1720), Brit. Mus. (N.R.), 357 b, 31/73.

the names are those that appeared in 1720 not as brokers but as underwriters and merchants.[1]

For the second half of the century, when they were in their prime, it is interesting to take those on Braund's books as a sample of the class. The occurrence of the names of many of the most distinguished merchants of London in the risks Braund wrote for these brokers, suggests that they are important and representative. Not counting merchants and their clerks who dealt directly with Braund (and these though not numerous, fifteen in all, were always on his books) he dealt, between 1741 and 1774, with seventy-six of them, whose names are given in the appendix.[2] Of these only a minute proportion, on the whole the newer firms, are entered in the London directories as insurance-brokers from the beginning. Charles Child in 1744, and J. Wilson, J. Gay, S. Haynes, Jonathan Hooper, and Thomas and Henry Hayes in 1738 are the only examples before 1750, and even then Charles Child is entered under that title only three years after Braund began to deal with him.[3] The others, even those who, as we can see from the Braund papers, were already doing considerable work in insurance broking, stand in the early directories either as merchants, sometimes merchants and insurers, as warehousemen, Blackwell-Hall factors, or general brokers. Richard Butler, of Butler and Mauger, began life as a ship's captain, and Dick, Angerstein's first partner, as a ship-owner and merchant. These were the men who, not at first office-keepers, began to 'make policies sometimes' and who concentrated more and more on the business as its scope extended. By the 'sixties and 'seventies, however active they may still have been in other lines of business,

---

[1] Special Report of 1720, cited *supra.*

[2] Appendix IV.

[3] By 1760, seventeen of the seventy-six firms examined are entered in the directories as insurance-brokers. It is interesting to compare the number of firms entered as insurance office-keepers in Kent's Directories of 1738 and 1759. In the former there are only five firms : John Gay, Lombard Street ; T. & H. Hayes, Cornhill ; S. Haynes, Change Alley ; J. Hooper, Change Alley ; J. Wilson, behind the Royal Exchange. (William Braund dealt with all of them, and with seventeen others, in 1741.) In 1759 there are forty entries, four of which are entered with other occupations as well. (Only sixteen of these are in Braund's books.)

they are, with few exceptions, entered in the directories simply as insurance-brokers.

This great importance of the broker not only arose out of the conditions of the agglomeration of Lloyd's, but made it inevitable that brokers should play a large part in any further development. Though there was, no doubt, some bitterness among the underwriters branded by brokers as 'bad and litigious', bitterness such as Weskett showed, and though in the next fifty years the unofficial dominance of the brokers was to go down before the growing organization of the underwriters as a body, brokers and underwriters never formed into opposing camps. Neither side was sufficiently specialized or exclusive for such a development, and the elasticity of rapid growth precluded consolidation of power in the hands of any one group of persons. The growth of organization within Lloyd's was thus neither one of the underwriter for protection against the broker, nor of the broker to maintain the strength of his position against the underwriter, but of underwriters and brokers together in the interest of the credit of the market. In such a combination the brokers, by their personal eminence, inevitably played a very prominent part.

As late as 1780 it was still not certain whence the insurance organization of the future would proceed. In 1780 it seemed at least as possible that the greater solidarity which every one admitted to be desirable should come from the voluntary organization running Lloyd's Register, as from the unorganized coffee-house as a whole.[1] But there had already come into existence an institution which was to prove more flexible and capable of growth. It came into existence when in 1769 a new Lloyd's Coffee-house seceded from the old, and, after some years of conflict, was successful in replacing it. In the New Lloyd's Coffee-house only members were admitted, and the members exercised some control over its management through a committee. This committee proved the nucleus of all future growth in organization.

In both institutions, Lloyd's Register and New Lloyd's,

---

[1] Weskett, op. cit., 'Preliminary Discourse', xxxv seq. (this discourse was published separately a year before the main work).

the brokers were prominent. Among the subscribers to the Register, the first list of whom is not found till 1778–9, comprising then about 130 names,[1] and in the list of the seventy-nine bondholders for the New Lloyd's Coffee-house of 1771,[2] where are to be found the names of the best known of the younger element of the London insurance market, the names of men primarily known as brokers are prominent. The committees elected by the latter during these years of change up to the end of the century were dominated by two men, Kuyck van Mierop and Angerstein, of whom the former was a merchant and underwriter ; but the latter was a man who, however prominent as an underwriter, reached this position through his importance at the same time as a broker. Indeed, the very split between new and old Lloyd's represents also a split in the broker interest. It has been assumed that the growth of gambling and undesirable dealing in the old coffee-house was the cause of the secession. Such things probably played their part, but there may have been a different cause. It is significant that the strong broker interest represented in the split is not that of the old broker firms who had been doing the business of the leading London merchants for the past twenty-five years, and whose businesses still existed under their own or their successors' control, but on the whole of a newer interest, supported by merchants who had risen later to prominence. Thus, though there were exceptions, it tended to represent the breach between the younger interests and the older, and not merely between the more reputable and the disreputable.

Yet the strength of the broker had passed its apex by the end of the century, and power to control the market was beginning to break down. By the end of the century, partly to gain the advantage of the discount which had by

[1] *Annals of Lloyd's Register*, op. cit., p. 12.

[2] Quoted in full by F. Martin, op. cit., p. 147. The bondholders were not by any means all the subscribers, who by enrolling themselves began the conception of membership of Lloyd's. There was at this time a considerable movement among the coffee-houses used for specialized purposes to limit their membership in this way. A complete list of members survives in the first minute book of Lloyd's drawn up in 1800. There is also a printed copy of which a copy exists in the Guildhall Library. Unfortunately no dates of entry or any other particular is given for those who became members from 1771 to 1800.

that time become so heavy, the merchant was finding it profitable to deal directly with the underwriters, either in person or through a clerk, particularly when insuring for a foreign correspondent, when this added greatly to his commission. A merchant thus assembled a number of underwriters whom he knew and trusted (often the more because they were themselves merchants from whom in other trading activities he had something in the nature of securities). This method of business, though strongly disliked by the brokers, had been known before (such prominent merchants as James Bourdieu are found using it by the mid-century), but it had greatly increased. By 1810 many witnesses stated that scarcely more than a third of their business passed though the hands of the brokers.[1] This loss of functional importance was intensified, more-over, by a great increase in the size of the market at the end of the century, which would in any case have made the brokers' duties far more complicated, and by the fact that, as the great underwriter developed, the broker made no simi-lar advance. The personal position of the broker began to alter signally. In the new days of insurance fortunes, men seldom retired rich on their brokerage, and, with the notable exception of Angerstein, they tended to be swamped beneath the flood of new capital which poured into the market and changed its conditions. There can be no doubt that by 1810 the brokers were behindhand in the pros-perity of the insurance market. In a period of unusual difficulties their intermediate position laid them dangerously open to risks, and in the fluctuations of war and inflation they found the burden of guaranteed premiums very heavy. High as were their brokerage and discount, there was found in the evidence before the committee of 1810 no underwriter who complained of unnecessary imposition. ' I would rather begin the world again ', said a broker witness, ' and pursue any other line.'[2] It was not the point of view of the mid-eighteenth century. The extreme

---

[1] 1810 Report, loc. cit., J. Fisher Throckmorton, Esq., underwriter, p. 91, says $\frac{2}{3}$ of his business done through brokers. J. Mavor, Esq., merchant and underwriter calculates $\frac{2}{3}$ of his, p. 95. George Shedden, Esq., underwriter thinks less than $\frac{1}{2}$ his business done through brokers, p. 101. Some witnesses do none through brokers.

[2] 1810 Report, loc., cit. p. 76.

personal depression of the broker was, it is true only temporary, but it reflected a permanent loss of functional control. From that time on this decline of the prominence of the broker is tacitly recognized in the growth of the organization of Lloyd's. Stage by stage, new and more elaborate controls and sanctions by committees and officials, representing the underwriting members as a whole, grew up by the side of the old responsibilities of the broker, and, as the bill-broker rose, the close organization of New Lloyd's quietly put aside the earlier power of the insurance-broker.

William Braund was probably as representative an underwriter as could be found for the years 1741–74. He was a steady but by no means a great underwriter, and the number and value of his risks, even at the height of his activities in the years around 1764, was less than half that of John Janson in 1805, which Danson takes to be characteristic of a man beginning business at that time. Forty years, however, had made a great difference in the scale of insurance dealings, and the regularity of Braund's relations, and the respectability of the brokers with whom he dealt, show him as a sound underwriter, who must have played his part, though never a great one, in the small knot which formed then the centre of Lloyd's. His attendance at Lloyd's, either in person or through a substitute,[1] must have been continuous, for at least from 1759, when his accounts become complete, there are no months of the year in which his underwriting activities cease. At the seasons when numbers of underwriters were in the habit of absenting themselves from the Coffee-house, both for a holiday and to avoid the difficulties of a period of premium adjustment, Braund's books show on the contrary, like those of greater men, a big increase in the risks underwritten—a sure sign of one of the ' old standards ' of Lloyd's who

---

[1] There is no reference in all his accounts to any one who might have acted as a substitute for him at Lloyd's. Diligent attendance at the Coffee-house was held to be essential to an underwriter. In John Eliot's first year at the business his uncle reproached him for leaving Town. ' If thou intends to carry business on, and more especially to be an Insurer, diligence is absolutely proper to be kept to : for an underwriter ought always to attend and be in the way.' *Eliot Papers*, op. cit., i. 45.

'always remain in their places'.[1] Even at the end of the
century it was still quite common for underwriting to take
place in other coffee-houses and for merchants to underwrite even in their own offices, but this tended to be
specialized work, and both the names and the number of
brokers with whom Braund dealt and the variety of his
risks make it quite clear that he must have underwritten at
Lloyd's itself. It is more doubtful what happened to him
when the split came between the old and new Lloyd's in
1769, which opened the way to new developments. He
was by then old and diminishing the scope of his business,
and the bad feeling and difficulties which accompanied the
split may have hastened his retirement. His name does
not appear among the seventy-nine bondholders for New
Lloyd's in 1771, nor on the list of early members of
Lloyd's, though those of ten brokers and two merchants
with whom he had had dealings are among the former.
He continued to write, though not extensively, with three
members. However, most of his diminishing business was
with the broker firms with whom he had long had business
relations, in some cases for thirty years, and with whom his
connexion had been most continuous. These names are not
to be found among the subscribers to New Lloyd's. For
Braund's place lay with the old rather than the new, and
he died in 1774 with the seventeen risks he had on hand, to
the value of £3,750, all at Old Lloyd's.

His underwriting activities fall into four main periods,
partly in a natural way, partly on account of the manner in
which his accounts have come down to us.

The first is that of 1741–58, a period beginning in one
war and ending in another, only a unity in that his
accounts are here very incomplete.

The second, 1758–63, is the time of his war-time activities, when, not yet a specialized underwriter, he was
nevertheless underwriting considerable sums under
the stimulus of the great war premiums.

The third, 1763–6, is the peace, in which premiums fell,
but Braund increased the scope of his activities and
concentrated almost entirely on underwriting.

[1] 1810 Report, Evidence of Moses Getting, p. 86.

The fourth, 1766–74, is the period of his old age, in which he began to cut down his commitments until he underwrote his last risk in January 1774.

Of the first of these periods only a general impression can be gained. Nothing can be said of the rate of premiums and little of the extent of Braund's business. We can form the fullest picture of the first year, 1741, an important and disastrous one, when the weight of misfortunes of the maritime war with Spain, the war of Jenkins' Ear, was being felt by the English insurance market. It seems probable that Braund's insurance business was then new. It may indeed, like that of so many others, have begun with the war. He had not yet evolved his later method of combining his insurance and other trading accounts, and (as was commonly done only by underwriters whose need of capital was urgent) he exacted payment of the balance of his premiums from the brokers early in the ensuing year with a punctuality he never insisted on later. These balances were large enough to show that he had been doing steady business with some brokers at least during the preceding year. In January he received:

£150 from N. Fletcher.
£16 „ S. Nicholson.
£100 „ J. Hooper.

and on 28 February:

£100 from J. Wilson.
£400 „ J. Crichlowe.

During 1741 twenty-two brokers are mentioned, several of them well-known men with whom he kept up a connexion for many years; Charles Child, Nathaniel Fletcher, Richard Madan, Jacob Espinoza, Phineas Serra, John and Travers Richards, and Wilson and Eastland.

The conditions of his business throughout this first year can be best judged, in the imperfection of his accounts, by his monthly entries of averages and losses in the journal. The losses mirror the misfortunes of that disastrous year. They were:

| February, 4 | June, 1 | September, 3 | November, 22 |
| March, 2 | July, 1 | October, 2 | *Total* 35. |

The abnormal conditions of the time show themselves in
the fact that there were fewer claims for average than for
loss, a condition only common in time of war; 32 claims
for average as against 35 losses.   In the fatal month of
November there were only 14 claims for average as against
22 for losses, caused no doubt by capture by the Spaniards.
Some of the ships concerned were bound for Oporto, others
probably were at that time of year returning from the West
Indies.   It is significant that next winter he reinsured a ship
from St. Kitt's to London (a proceeding not yet declared
illegal by statute) for the high premium of 40 per cent.

In the more settled years of 1742–3 the information is
less, but his business was apparently shaken by the misfortunes of 1741. He appears to have relied on his less
perilous activities as a merchant. Except for a few return
premiums, and the one reinsurance noted above, no business
is recorded, and the names of only six brokers occur in the
accounts for these two and a half years.   In 1744 the gap
in the accounts comes, and no more information is obtain-
able until the cash book opens in 1747.

In this the evidence is even less complete than in the
journal, for no note is made in the cash book, naturally,
of any transactions not based on cash.   It is clear, nevertheless, from the beginning that Braund's business is once
again on a good footing.   Once again he gets payments on
balance from brokers, and to a considerably greater sum,
and he does not now demand them until later in the year,
sometimes as late as June or July. In 1749, for example,
he received from the brokers the following balances :

January 18th   £200 from Wilson and Eastland.
    „   20th   £21 18s. 6d. from M. da Paiba.
    „   26th   £30 from W. Deacon.
    „   27th   £12 5s. from P. Serra.
February 14th   £100 from Fletcher and Cole.
April 13th   £292 8s. 3d. from J. Gay.
June —   £50 from D. Solomon.
    „   £300 from C. Child.

When it is borne in mind that the war-time premiums
have gone, these sums show all the more to what extent
his business had increased.   They are the only means by

which at this period the prosperity of his business can be estimated. It is not even possible to gauge the numbers of his losses and the claims upon him for average, since these are only to be found in the cash book in the comparatively rare cases when Braund is dealing directly with a merchant without the use of a broker as an intermediary, or when the balance in the hands of the broker is insufficient to cover the claim. Braund paid no more than nine of such claims between 1747 and 1758. The increase of his business is also reflected in the growth in the number of brokers with whom he dealt. In 1759 there are twenty-eight on his books, and the numbers are steadily growing.[1]

The opening of 1758 begins a new stage in our understanding of his insurance. It comes, moreover, at a time when Braund had already taken the first step in his progress from the ranks of the merchant to those of the specialized dealer in finance. He had already left the wholesale woollen trade with Portugal and begun the bullion venture which continued until the end of 1762. In 1758 the new journal takes up the account of his activities, and more fully than the old; the ledger is also available, and by 1759 follow the journals of risks which make all clear. Braund was by that time once again concerned with war and war premiums, and though the bullion trade was absorbing most of his capital the volume of his insurance business remained steadily large. The following table shows the sums taken in premiums during these years:

	£	s.	d.
1758	11,377	18	5
1759	9,599	3	11
1760	7,282	8	5
1761	7,009	14	8
1762	9,032	1	3
1763	4,255	13	10

It is now, for the first time, possible to see the full workings of Braund's business, and it is interesting to examine its scope and nature. He mixed his risks, as Angerstein boasted men learned to do at Lloyd's, and covered what would appear to be a very wide range of insurance business

[1] These figures are taken from the journal of risks.

for that time. Angerstein spoke of the vagaries of the man who would take a dangerous West Indian risk, but could not be induced to consider an English coasting one. Braund was not such a man. Ships and their cargoes of timber, hemp, and tar from the Baltic, and especially Riga and St. Petersburg, are common right up to December, though some of the ports might be closed by ice. All forms of American and West Indian risks are to be found, both out and back, though the outward risks are often the trading voyages of the triangular trade, from England to the Slave Coast and on to the slave-owning colonies. Spanish, Portuguese, and Italian risks are common; the Near East was represented by Smyrna and Scanderoon (Alexandretta), and Braund underwrote a number of bottomry and respondentia bonds on East Indiamen, the ordinary credit instrument of owners or captains trying to raise capital. The Canaries, in connexion with the wine trade, were another fairly common risk. Dutch risks, on the other hand, are found so seldom that, in view of the large volume of trade with Holland, serious competition from Amsterdam is suggested. The prominence of coastwise risks is important. Danson observed in the books of John Janson of 1805 that the number of coasting risks much diminished in the summer months. He remarked:

'It may be that the Underwriter whose work is before me had not a full share of this class of risk. But the smaller number of risks in summer seems to have been constant. It may have arisen, partly, from a greater disposition of the assured to take their own risk when damage to cargo, not coverable by insurance, was less likely.'[1]

Braund's papers show, however, a reversed position. The coasting risks of the summer months greatly outnumber those of the winter. There is no justification for believing that even in 1759, still less in 1805, insurance was not regularly used in the coastwise trade, though there is not enough evidence definitely to prove this. Cross risks are continuously found, sometimes of the most complicated nature, and they justify the boast of Lloyd's that they had developed to a very remarkable degree in this often dan-

[1] Danson, op. cit., p. 40.

gerous and obscure form of insurance. These risks may be divided into three classes. First come European risks, including risks between Europe and the Far East. Then there are risks in the Far East alone. These were few, but the local Indian markets, which were well developed for this form of insurance by 1810,[1] had as yet scarcely come into existence. Finally, there were risks in American waters, or for the crossing to Europe; these were the most numerous of them all. They often take the form of complicated trading voyages, many of them from the Newfoundland fisheries to the markets of Portugal or the Mediterranean. Of time risks there are always a few, some on lives (some of them mere wager policies), some on ships at the Newfoundland fisheries, packet boats, or privateers on cruise during the war.

These widely ranging risks were undertaken for a variety of merchants. Apart from the numbers of foreign firms who are on his books, there occur most of the names prominent in London commerce and in merchant politics of the mid-eighteenth century. There is Sir William Baker, the ally in the City of the Duke of Newcastle, who insured his American ventures at first through the broking firm of Richard Madan, then from 1765 through a clerk, George Hogsflesh; Samuel Touchet; James Bourdieu, who speculated in sugar prices on the Amsterdam market, and who always insured directly through his clerk (later his partner), Samuel Chollett; and also Sir Samuel Fludyer, the Fonnereaus, Fisher and Pearse (the successors of Brice Fisher), Barlow Trecothick, and many others. The brokers with whom Braund was connected were also men of importance, and include among their number the name of Angerstein, which was to become more important in the future. His relations with these brokers varied from the writing of an occasional risk to a close permanent connexion. He underwrote on the office account of four brokers,

---

[1] Report of 1810, pp. 21-2. Evidence of George Simson, M.P., of the firm of Bruce, De Ponthieu & Co., and (p. 26 seq.) William Manning of the firm of Porcher & Co., &c. Some facilities for insurance had existed, however, for those sending valuables from India. In 1777 Captain McPherson writes from India, 'I have not insured the above gold'. *Soldiering in India 1764–1786*, ed. W. C. McPherson, p. 318.

Eastland and Lewis, Richard Madan, Jacob Espinoza, and, for more than thirty years, of Andrew Moffatt, with whom his business was for every month among the heaviest on his books.

Wide as was the scope of his underwriting and many as were his business relations in it, one must not assume that it was necessarily entirely representative. The connexions of his brokers, and still more his personal connexions, must have influenced the nature of his business. In the first place, his contact with Portugal, kept up even after he had left the trade, through his nephew Benjamin Branfill, probably accounts for some of the importance of Spanish and Portuguese risks; in the second place, his close connexions with the East India shipping interests must be responsible for some of the many risks written on bottomry and respondentia bonds on East Indiamen. This should be borne in mind when the following analysis of the distribution of his risks during the year 1759 is read. There is nothing with which it can be compared before 1805. It is simply an analysis of one man's risks in the mid-eighteenth century:

Risks.	Jan.	Feb.	Mar.	April	May	June	July	Aug.	Sept.	Oct.	Nov.	Dec.	Total.	
England—N. American Colonies.														
Out	6	4	18	9	10	4	10	19	8	15	8	2	113 }	163
Back	3	3	6	1	4	2	4	5	4	16	1	1	50 }	
Ireland—N. American Colonies.														
Out	1	..	2	..	5	2	..	5	1	3	1	..	20 }	22
Back	1	..	..	..	..	..	..	..	1	..	..	..	2 }	
Scotland—N. American Colonies.														
Out	..	1	1	..	..	..	..	1	..	..	..	..	3 }	3
Back	..	..	..	..	..	..	..	..	..	..	..,	..	}	
England—Jamaica.														
Out	7	1	2	..	1	1	1	2	1	5	4	..	25 }	64
Back	5	1	2	1	5	2	10	9	3	1	..	..	39 }	
Ireland—W. Indies.														
Out	1	1	2	2	1	..	2	..	1	1	2	..	13 }	14
Back	..	..	..	..	..	..	1	..	..	..	..	..	1 }	

Risks.	*Jan.*	*Feb.*	*Mar.*	*April*	*May*	*June*	*July*	*Aug.*	*Sept.*	*Oct.*	*Nov.*	*Dec.*	*Total.*
Scotland—W. Indies.													
Out	2	..	..	..	..	..	..	..	1	2	..	..	5}
Back	..	..	..	..	..	..	..	1	..	..	..	..	1} 6
England—all other W. Indies.													
Out	4	..	8	..	2	..	5	10	3	4	3	3	42}
Back	..	..	..	..	5	2	2	3	..	8	..	1	21} 63
England—E. Indies.													
Out	2	..	4	3	5	..	..	..	..	..	5	2	21}
Back	2	2	2	1	8	..	..	..	..	3	2	3	23} 44
England—Spain and Portugal.													
Out	5	4	7	5	14	3	7	8	8	12	9	12	94}
Back	9	2	3	4	5	3	2	1	2	7	2	7	47} 141
England—Italy.													
Out	10	3	6	..	2	1	5	..	5	3	4	2	41}
Back	1	5	2	1	..	3	3	2	1	4	2	3	27} 68
England—Holland and Flanders.													
Out	3	2	1	..	1	2	4	5	7	1	3	..	29}
Back	1	..	..	..	..	1	..	3	2	4	1	..	12} 41
England—Baltic.													
Out	..	..	..	..	5	2	5	..	2	13	3	2	32}
Back	..	2	..	2	5	7	1	6	12	14	2	3	54} 86
England—Near East.													
Out	1	..	..	..	..	..	..	..	2	4	1	3	11}
Back	2	..	3	..	..	..	..	1	..	..	..	..	6} 17
England—Hamburg, Emden, &c.													
Out	..	2	..	2	2	..	2	1	1	1	..	..	11}
Back	..	1	..	..	1	..	1	1	..	..	..	..	4} 15
Ireland, Channel and Coast.	8	6	14	2	13	11	9	17	9	11	7	6	113
Time	6	1	4	2	4	5	8	2	2	3	2	2	41
Cross risks.													
(a) Europe	9	9	3	3	6	8	1	10	4	9	2	1	65
(b) Europe—American waters, or American waters alone . .	9	15	8	6	11	14	18	17	18	17	11	5	149
(c) Europe—Far East, or Far East alone . .	1	2	..	2	1	2	1	..	..	4	1	1	15
Miscellaneous . . .	4	4	8	4	5	5	8	7	8	18	6	3	80

One may compare briefly the distribution of Braund's risks with those of John Janson in 1805.[1] The latter may be summarized as follows:

Total.   Over 3,000.

Canada, U.S.A., and Newfoundland . . .	470
West Indies	432
East Indies	76
Gibraltar and Mediterranean[2]	294
France, Spain, and Portugal	344
Tonningen, Emden, &c.	858
Baltic	359
Coasting	370
Time	51
Miscellaneous	45

From this list it may be seen that Janson was far less concerned in cross risks that Braund, for they are included apparently in his forty-five miscellaneous risks, while Braund in 1759 took 235 of them. Janson took proportionately more West Indian and Mediterranean risks, about the same proportion of North American and Newfoundland risks (Canada was, however, a new factor since 1759), a smaller proportion of Spanish, Portuguese, and East Indian risks, and a much greater proportion of Baltic risks. Emden and Tonningen are a new feature in Janson's accounts; these cities enjoyed in 1805 a quite new and temporary importance as almost the only ports of entry to the German markets which the Napoleonic conquests still left open to us. By 1805 the war had, on the other hand, stopped Dutch risks altogether. Janson's time risks are of much less importance to him than Braund's; his coasting risks are proportionately equal.

The importance of this underwriting business to Braund during the Seven Years War is shown not only by the increase in the risks he undertook but by the steadiness of his attendance at Lloyd's. The import of bullion was a

---

[1] Danson, op. cit., pp. 17–18.

[2] Under the heading of Mediterranean risks Danson includes Gibraltar and the Near East. My table divides the category Mediterranean into Italian and Near Eastern risks, but I include Gibraltar risks under Spain and Portugal. This is not of much importance as Braund underwrote few risks to and from Gibraltar.

purely financial activity, and free from the business claims
he had to meet earlier as an exporting merchant, in these
years when premiums were high and dangers great he
underwrote daily with the exception of the week-ends and
Mondays, and was able to give constant attention to his
business at Lloyd's. During these years the vicissitudes of
the Seven Years War as well as Braund's fortunes can be
followed in his insurance accounts. They can be seen in
the numbers of his risks and in the sums of premiums,
affected now less by winter and summer than by the actions
of the French, and in 1762 by the new and in many fields
more dangerous menace of the Spaniards. They can be
seen too in the reserves he provided each year in his ledger
against the dangers of the next and in the sums paid for
losses, and their high proportion to those paid for averages,
which indicate clearly enough the need for the caution
which his reserves showed. The following tables indicate
these conditions for the two years 1759 and 1762, the one
at the height of the French menace, the other under the
added shadow of Spain.

	1759	1762
No. of risks . . .	1,210	857
Sum of premiums . .	£9,599 3s. 11d.	£9,032 1s. 3d.
Sum of reserves in ledger .	£6,391 8s. 9d.	£4,411 7s. 2d.
Sum carried in ledger to profit and loss . .	£500	£2,500
No. of losses . . .	43	19
No. of averages . . .	39	35
Average written on each risk	roughly £145	roughly £144

These figures bring out certain points; in the first place,
although the number of risks he wrote in 1762 is only
about 70 per cent. of the number written in 1759, and the
average amount written on each risk remains constant, the
sum of the premiums received in 1762 is only about 6 per
cent. less than that received in 1759. This is the result of
the rise in the level of premiums brought about by the en-
trance of Spain into the war. In the second place, they bring
out the great fluctuation of the sums which Braund considered at the end of each year he could safely estimate as net
gain. Though these figures depended on the circumstances

of the moment, such estimates are of some value when spread over several years. During the years of war, from 1758 to 1762, they stand in the following proportionate relation to each other:

	1758	*1759*	*1760*
Profit and loss .	£1,500	£500	nil
Balance for reserve	£6,629 17s. 1d.	£6,391 8s. 9d.	£299 13s. 7d.

	1761	*1762*
Profit and loss . . .	nil	£2,500
Balance for reserve .	£3,409 8s. 11d.	£4,411 7s. 2d.

It is clear the heaviest strain of the war fell on Braund in 1760 and 1761. These were the years of the war during which he underwrote least, and in which he put most into the bullion trade. In the greater dangers of 1762 he definitely gained, for he seems to have enjoyed surprisingly good luck. Although all premiums were raised to meet the Spanish menace, his own losses were no more than those due to wind and weather in the peace year of 1764.

Braund thus, to sum up, came through the war without any repetition of the disaster of his early war year of 1741. At the end of the war he was both richer than when he had entered it and more closely involved in the financial organization of London commerce. His importations of bullion ceased in 1762, and he thereby severed all connexion with foreign trade. He maintained his shipping interests, which are examined in a later chapter, but they were those rather of a capitalist investor than an *entrepreneur*. His chief use of his capital and his chief business activity was now his underwriting at Lloyd's alone. For some years he had been investing in land, as well as in stocks, and he now began to take an interest in his estate, for he had in 1762 joined the ranks of the well-to-do merchants whose country houses ringed London with continually growing villages, near enough to Town for their owners to ride easily into the City in summer.

Braund might, indeed, have justifiably retired from business altogether at this point. He was by 1763 sixty-seven years of age, solidly prosperous, of good reputation in the

City, unmarried, and with his capital entirely free. That he was still a man of vigour is suggested by the fact that he clearly entertained no such thoughts. In the third period of his career as an underwriter, the post-war period of lowered premiums and a changed estimation of every type of risk, he now extended his business with skill and address. The fluctuations of the premiums, as they stagger towards normal, show how necessary this was. He became at this time, it seems plain, a more important man in the Coffee-house. His risks grew bigger as their numbers increased; to his old brokers, with whom he now did more business than before, he added new brokers, some occasionally, a few regularly, and his profits, although they remained some-what below those he earned at the peak of his war gains, were steady and satisfactory. The following figures show his profits and reserves during these years:

	1763	1764
Profit and loss	£1,500	£1,800
Balance for reserve	£1,626 15s. 5d.	£2,513 6s. 9d.

	1765	1766
Profit and loss	£1,000	£1,000
Balance for reserve	£1,984 4s. 6d.	£2,133 9s. 7d.

His business for 1764, when the readjustments of the return to peace had been made, can be seen in the follow-ing tables:

No. of risks	1,389
Sum of premiums	£5,099 10s. 1d.
Sum of reserves in ledger	£2,513 6s. 9d.
Sum carried in ledger to profit and loss	£1,800
No. of payments for averages	67 (the majority extremely
No. of losses	18 [small sums)
Average written on each risk	about £163

These are the first years of peace for which the accounts are complete. In them can be seen the level of premiums when not disturbed by war, and the level can be compared with those given by Malynes for 1622, Nicholas Magens for 1753, and Danson for 1816.

COMPARATIVE TABLE OF PREMIUMS, FROM AND TO LONDON*

Percentage.

	Malynes, 1622.	Magens, 1753. Summer	Magens, 1753. Winter	Braund, 1764.	Danson, 1816.
Middleburg	} 3 out and home. Amsterdam is quoted instead of Rotterdam and Dieppe added.	} 1 out and home	} 1½–2 out and home	London—Holland Out { summer, £1; winter, £1½ } Home { summer, £1; winter, £1½–2 }	} Germany, Holland, and France without Straits Out Home } 1·04
Rotterdam					
Edinburgh					
Hamburg	—	—	—	London—Hamburg Out { summer, 1 guinea; winter, 2½ guineas } Home { summer, 1 guineas; winter, 1½–5 guinea }	—
Rouen	—	—	—		—
Bordeaux	} 4 out and home	} 1¼ ,,	} 2–2¼ ,,	—	} Germany, Holland, and France without Straits Out Home } 1·04
Rochelle					
Lubeck				—	Russia, Norway, Sweden, Baltic { Out 1·8; Home 3·4 }
Copenhagen (in Malynes 'Denmark')					
Lisbon	} 5 ,,	} 1¼ ,,	} 1¼–1½ ,,	London—Lisbon Out { summer, 1 guinea } Home { winter, £1½ }	Spain, Portugal, and Mediterranean { Out 2·1; Home 2·56 }
Biscay					
Ireland	5 ,,	1¼ ,,	1¼–1½ ,,	Out { autumn (no summer risks), £1¼ } Home { winter, £1½ }	—

78

				London quotations	Danson's grouping	
Danzig Riga	5 ,, Also Barbary, Revel, and Sweden	1½ ,,	2½–3 ,,	London—Riga Range from £1¼ (May) to 8 guineas (November)	Russia, Norway, Sweden, Baltic	OUT 1·8 HOME 3·4
Cadiz (in Malynes Seville is quoted instead) Gibraltar Malaga	6–7 out and home Also the 'Islands'	1¼ ,,	1¼–1 ,,	London—Cadiz and Malaga OUT { summer, 1 guinea HOME { winter, £1¼–£1½	Spain, Portugal, and Mediterranean	OUT 2·1 † HOME 2·56
Livorno Civita Vecchia	8–9 out and home	1¼ ,,	1½–2 ,,	London—Leghorn and Civita Vecchia OUT { all the year round £1½ HOME {	Spain, Portugal, and Mediterranean	OUT 2·1 † HOME 2·56
Venice	10 ,,	1½ ,,	1¾–2 ,,	Insufficient data	—	
Archangel (in Malynes 'Russia')	9 ,,	2½ ,,	3 ,,	—	—	‡
East Indies. Out and home ,, ,, OUT ,, ,, HOME	15–20 — —	8 — —	8 — —	6 guineas (June and Sept.) to 7 guineas £3½–4 guineas £4–4 guineas		4·76
Jamaica. OUT ,, HOME	— —	—	—	OUT, £3, all the year. HOME, £5–£8		
North America. including Newfoundland. OUT HOME	— —	—	—	OUT { £2½ all year round HOME {	British North America and Newfoundland	2·4 2·4
Coastwise	—	—	—	£1–£1¼ varying not with seasons but with distance		0·97

* Magens deliberately fitted his classification of premiums into that which Malynes had used, for purposes of comparison. Danson has grouped his voyages differently, so that comparison is difficult. I have tried to include his quotation where it can be useful, and to put my own into the same form.
† The way in which Danson groups together 'Spain, Portugal, and the Mediterranean' makes his figures here not very useful for comparison.
‡ Danson gives a quotation for 'Russia, Norway, Sweden, and Baltic'. It is probable that he was thinking only of the Russian Baltic ports and not of Archangel. The same may apply to Malynes. Braund sometimes underwrote risks to and from Archangel, but none occurs in this year.

79

The third stage of Braund's underwriting career, his activity after the war, did not, however, last very long. By 1766 his age was evidently pressing on him, and he must have felt that at seventy his efforts might relax. In that year he closed his accounts with a number of brokers and ceased to underwrite for others, and few new names take their place. Though he continued to write fairly extensively with a few of the brokers with whom he had long been closely connected, in particular with Moffatt (John, who had now succeeded Andrew), he attended Lloyd's less frequently, and by 1770 only underwrote three or four days a month. In 1766 he underwrote only 548 risks in all. In 1769 there was still a further drop, possibly on account of the breach between the old and new Lloyd's, though he continued to deal with a few of the seceders. By his death in 1774 he had only a shadow of his business. Very likely, indeed, he no longer went himself to Lloyd's. Since 1772 he had transactions with Moffatt alone, and it seems very probable that Moffatt acted during these years as his agent.[1] His last risk was underwritten on 10 January, six months before his death.

Thus the insurance business of William Braund, the climax of his slow progress along the road to pure finance followed by so many merchants of his time, faded away to its end, and, at the expense of a few reinsurances by his executors at Old Lloyd's, every sign of his activity passed as promptly and easily away as it has done with others of his calling. He had seen two wars, and a great growth of insurance; but he died a few years before the new impetus of the American War of Independence; he had seen the growth of Old Lloyd's and the secession of the New, but none of the possibilities latent in the closer cohesion of the latter, and belonged, in short, essentially to an age that was, as regards insurance, formative and not a realization.

[1] A broker giving evidence before the 1810 Committee said that he was doing this for an underwriter. *Report*, p. 76.

IV

WILLIAM BRAUND AND THE EAST INDIA SHIPPING INTEREST

I. *The East India Shipping Interest*

WILLIAM BRAUND had his ventures in the Portugal woollen trade and the bullion trade, and underwrote his risks at Lloyd's. He would not, however, have been a representative London merchant of that time had he not touched two other spheres of activity; the concerns, political and speculative, of the East India Company, and those of the London shipping interest, which had become so important in the eighteenth-century rise of the mercantile marine. He did both, and in ways which were closely interconnected. Besides his other shipping concerns, Braund was a member, and (since he was for eight years a Director of the East India Company) an important member, of the famous East India shipping interest. This close body was then in its prime. It was scarcely yet troubled by the attacks, political and economic, which were to harass it during the last quarter of the century, when it shared in the dissolution of a dying East Indian system.

Braund's business in the East India shipping was not undertaken alone. He was here acting in close connexion with his younger brother Samuél, who took the active part in these concerns until his retirement from business in 1760. He is a dimmer figure than William; he held no offices in the City, and his will cannot be traced, but he may well have been prominent in the London commercial world of the time, for he was one of the principal ships' husbands in that oligarchic East India shipping interest during the 'forties and 'fifties, when it was at the height of its unchallenged power. That he and his brother William were working very closely together is shown not only by the fact that his ship books, on which this examination is based, were kept among the accounts of the latter (for this might have been an accident), but also that the cash payments and receipts which Samuel's business entailed were habitually made by William.

The shipping concerns of the Braunds can only be understood as part of the complicated mechanism of the East
India shipping interest, and in this is their sole importance.
Before their papers can be used in any way, therefore, it is
necessary to investigate the nature of one of the strangest
products of this age of association, the East India shipping
interest.

The East India Company shipping system was, from a
purely commercial point of view, no more than a special
instance of the ordinary system of the time, for with few
exceptions the East India Company hired its ships and
actually had a by-law prohibiting the expenditure of the
money in the Company treasury on the building of ships
for trade.[1] The eighteenth-century system of ship-owning,
of which it formed a part, was substantially that which can
be traced far back in the history of medieval shipping; the
sharing of ownership in parts among a number of independent men. It was the same system, much simplified, which
was regulated by the statute of 1833-4,[2] and this system
continued to predominate through much of the nineteenth
century, until the limited liability company arose to take the
place of the older association of owners. It was a method
which reflected admirably, as did Lloyd's in another sphere,
both the individualism and the needs of co-operation of the
contemporary commercial organization.

By this system a number of merchants combined to build
or buy a ship, each accepting one or more shares, usually
expressed in the eighteenth century as sixteenths or thirty-
seconds, but by the statute of 1833-4 as sixty-fourths.[3]

---

[1] By-law, No. 8. See *By-Laws, Constitutions, Orders and Rules* . . . Printed
1774. This by-law confirmed a resolution of the Court of Directors of 8 Oct.
1697 (India Office: E. I. Co., Ct. Bk. 37, f. 404). Exception was made of small
boats, and in the later part of the century it was waived on several occasions. It
was later repealed. The original intention, as was pointed out, was to check the
Company's experiments in the past few years in the part-owning of ships. (See Ct.
Bk. 36, f. 264, 5 December 1694, &c.)

[2] 3 and 4 William IV, c. 55.

[3] In the seventeenth century ownership in shares appears to have been general
in the case of big ships, particularly in London. In the outports it was still unusual
(V. Barbour, ' Dutch and English Merchant Shipping in the Seventeenth Century ',
Econ. Hist. Rev., 1930). In the eighteenth century it seems to have become general
there too. (Wadsworth and Mann, op. cit., pp. 224-5.)

The number of owners was limited by the statute to thirty-two, but they appear rarely in the eighteenth century to reach such a number even in the case of the big East Indiamen. The part owners subscribed for the costs of building, equipping, and repairing the ship according to their proportionate share ; could sell the share, insure it, or mortgage it, and received dividends on its profits in the same proportion. Their position approximated in many ways to that of members of a joint stock association, for they were liable to calls on their capital, had a right to the proceeds of the enterprise, and, like a joint stock company, they decided their policy in general meetings, usually at some well-known tavern, such as the *Fleece*.

For purposes of organization one of their number was, by the eighteenth century, chosen as the managing-owner, agent, or, as he was usually called, 'ship's husband'. His duties were by Samuel Braund's time well established by custom, reinforced a little by decisions at law. He was responsible for supervising the building, fitting, and sailing of the ship, and had to keep complete accounts, with which were incorporated those kept by the master and purser during the voyage. These he presented at a meeting of the owners at the end of each voyage.[1] The origin of the position of ship's husband was not very remote. In the early seventeenth century it is clear from the contemporary books of sea law that the master undertook himself most of the functions later carried out by the husband.[2] It is noteworthy that the *Oxford English Dictionary* can find no reference to the term 'ship's husband' earlier than 1730–6, though there is no doubt that the position had by then become well known. It is of interest for this study that the East India Company did more than any other body to develop the position of the husband.

The position of husband developed because it had certain obvious conveniences. The dual interests of master

---

[1] In the case of short voyages, e.g. ships in the Portugal trade, the meeting was held annually.

[2] As in 1665 when the Committee for Shipping arranged the freights with Henry Dacres and other commanders. (*Calender of the Court Minutes of the East India Company*, vii. 369.)

and owners, mixed as they were (for the master was always a prominent owner), found recognition in shipping organization. The master, on his side, was protected by the merchant custom (not always accepted by English law) that no ship could be sold until after its first voyage. The custom suggests, as Lord Tenterden pointed out in his exposition of the law of shipping,[1] the preponderating importance the master usually enjoyed among the owners before the rise of the husband, as the active *entrepreneur* of the business. Such a position he might maintain, except in the East India Company, even in the middle of the eighteenth century. In the Braund accounts we find such a man in Captain Benjamin Lyons, who was both master and husband of the merchantman *Braganza*. With the Company, on the other hand, it seems even in the seventeenth century to have been fairly common for the charter-parties, in which the terms of hire of ships were laid down, to be signed by representatives of the other owners as well as the master. By 1684 it had become established that the charter-party should be signed by two owners in addition to the master, who were often called the 'charter-party owners', or 'owners in charter-party'.[2]

The charter-party owners tended naturally to be men active among the owners in the business of the ship. It is easy to see how they achieved a special importance in the East India Company, for the owners of the ships it hired

---

[1] Op. cit., pp. 72–3.

[2] Ct. Bk. 33, f. 222. This was probably to avoid difficulties such as that which arose in 1668 when Captain Groome, commander of the *William and Mary*, signed a charter-party from the terms of which the rest of the owners tried to recede (*Cal. of Court Minutes*, vol. viii, p. 84). The names of the charter-party owners had to be given in to the Court of Directors and accepted. In 1703 (Ct. Bk. 41, ff. 352 and 163) the Directors decided that four names should be submitted, from whom they would choose two, but this was scarcely ever enforced. The Company made use of this regulation, after many years' disuse, to meet a special case in 1771 (Ct. Bk. 80, ff. 394–5) when it had quarrelled with the prominent ship's husband John Durand in the case of Captain Tod (see *infra*, p. 101). The other husbands at first protested against it as an innovation. *The Papers of Thomas Bowrey 1669–1713* (ed. R. C. Temple, Hakluyt Soc.; Series ii, vol. 58), Part II. p. 139, show that of the seven owners of the *Mary* galley, 1704–10, an interloper in the East Indies, Bowrey, who was the husband (the word is not used), and any two more of the subscribers 'who does not goe in the Ship', are to have power to do all the business of the ship. The two chosen do not, however, appear to take any active part in its management.

included among them many men of influence in the Company itself. The 'Committees', as the Directors of the Company were then called, tended from the beginning to push ships which they themselves owned for the Company's service. Hence the charter-party owner was often an important man, the true money power of the ship, and it is significant that, where a 'Committee' was an owner, the Company often directly consulted such a man on big matters concerning the ship, whatever representative they had been dealing with before.[1] Such men by no means necessarily took over the management of the ship, or the keeping of its accounts, in the way in which the husband later did. This they left on the whole to the master, who received from the Company what was due to the owners after every voyage and made up the accounts.

Nevertheless, the ship's husband as a type, or the 'managing-owner', as the East India Company began to call him, began to emerge among important owners, particularly among those who had themselves gained their wealth in the profitable position of commander of a ship in the East India Company's service. Eventually they were to monopolize the control of the ship in the name of the other owners, from whom they obtained a legal instrument in exchange for a bond.[2] There is no sign in the seventeenth-century East India Company records of any such instrument, but from an early date it is obvious that a few such important owners with big interests in the Company are managing their own ships, and one or two were important husbands like those found in the eighteenth century, concerned in a number of ships. Such a man was Captain, afterwards Sir William, Ryder,[3] the friend of Samuel Pepys.

---

[1] *Cal. of Court Minutes*, e.g. vol. vii, 1665, p. 163.

[2] But even towards the end of the eighteenth century the Company found it necessary to insist on such an instrument to avoid friction (*Printed Proceedings, Marine Miscellanies*, vol. 530, p. 304, 7 September 1786. Samuel Braund's accounts always contain an entry of 5*s*. for the costs of drawing one up, and a copy of one is to be found among his papers and is here printed, pp. 123–4.

[3] The first reference to him in the *Cal. Court Minutes* is in 1643, when he was master of the *Love*. In 1647 he was for the first of many times elected a 'Committee', and in 1662–3 and 1667–8 he was Deputy-Governor. He was knighted at the end of 1660. His shipping interests were extensive. His name occurs frequently in the *Cal. State Papers, Dom.*, between 1650 and 1671, in

Though the need for the managing-owner was more clearly apparent in the East India Company than elsewhere, the convenience of such an agent ashore became increasingly apparent in other forms of shipping, and in the early eighteenth century there are husbands to a very considerable proportion of other merchantmen as well as to every East Indiaman. In the East India shipping system, however, the importance they retained was unique.

From such a beginning, therefore, there had grown up by the eighteenth century, with the elaboration of London shipping, a small specialized class among the owners of ships. Certain men by experience and connexions were pointed out as suitable for the position of husband, and the class grew because it was something more than a class of managers, it was the initiating class among the owners. Often, as has been said, a master who had waxed rich and left the sea, it was this class of man who began to play the part of *entrepreneur* in the supply of shipping, who saw his opportunities, and who, sometimes alone, sometimes in conjunction with the master of the ship, brought together the other owners as virtually sleeping partners. The shipping interest of any town, even of London, was small and connected by many strands. Hence an important husband would be in charge of more ships than one, and in the East Indian shipping (where special circumstances were at work) a man might, like Samuel Braund, be husband to seven ships, or even, like a far greater husband of the 'sixties, Charles Raymond, to twenty-four.[1] His sphere of influence would reach to the famous Thames ship-builders, on the one hand, and the smallest purveyor of ship's biscuits, on the other. This position gave him a special importance, which compensated for the fact that, though the duties were fairly heavy, the direct payment was small.

connexion with Trinity House (of which he was Deputy-Master), with commerce (he was a Eastland merchant), and especially in connexion with his big contracts for ships' stores with the Navy; he died in 1669. See also Pepys *Diary* and *Letters*.

[1] C. Hardy, *A Register of Ships Employed in the Service of the United East India Company 1760-1810*. Revised and re-edited by Horatio Charles Hardy [his son], 1811. Gives the husbands of East Indiamen from 1760 onwards.

The first edition appears to be the anonymous work of the same title printed for Charles Hardy, Jerusalem Coffee-house, in 1798. A copy is preserved in the Goldsmiths' Library. There were several later editions.

Even an East India husband received until near the end of the eighteenth century only £50 a voyage, but it is easy to see that the indirect advantages were considerable. To consider only the more obvious aspects, there was all the influence which could be gained over, and the advantages which could be got from the tradesmen, often important firms, who were anxious to secure the contracts for supplying the ship's stores. Moreover, an arrangement was frequently made whereby the husband had a special claim to the patronage of the ship, a right always valuable, but which reached its height in the East India Company. The Company itself addressed husbands by the honorific title of Esquire in recognition of their rank.[1]

The conditions of the East India Company shipping show with unusual clearness, and in fact with exaggeration, the workings of the contemporary system of shipowning. The position of Samuel and William Braund and their associates may be used to illustrate this fact. In some ways the workings of the system of ownership may be studied in the Company shipping more closely than elsewhere, since relations with the Company rendered essential a clearer definition of functions and drew wider attention to questions of organization. In other ways, however, the position of the East India Company shipping was unique, for political factors had entered into every aspect of the Company's trade, and the 'shipping interest' had formed by the mid-eighteenth century a formidable monopoly within the Company itself. This fact is of cardinal importance in any treatment of East India shipping, as it is of Company politics. In 1783, nine years after William Braund's death had closed the Braund shipping ventures for ever, the Select Committee of the House of Commons stated (with some exaggeration) that the stock of the East India Company was held mainly for political reasons, on account of the close dependence of the Company on the Government. The Committee distinguished three main classes among these political proprietors, two of whom may be treated on similar lines, but one of which stands alone; those who

[1] *Letter to the Hon. the Board of Controul for India Affairs*, London, 1803. (Bodleian, Godwin Pamph. 1209 (8), p. 17.)

aspired to the Direction of the Company, and in consequence were careful to hold large blocks of stock in their own name and those of others; those who aimed at contracts from the Treasury, Admiralty, or Ordnance, and the clerks of the public offices, all men anxious to be useful to the Government in the Court of Proprietors ; and last, but for our purpose most important, the shipping interest 'a considerable proportion of the shipowners and tradesmen in London'.[1] This last class of proprietors stands alone, for it alone represents a commercial element in the midst of the political ones ; the shipping interest when it worked as such in a body, sought commercial ends by a steady use of political means. It was for this reason that these proprietors could claim, when ministerial influence was great, that they were the one independent party in the Company.[2] This was one of the grounds on which their enemies attacked 'an unauthorized and unchartered monopoly',[3] and this fact undoubtedly played a big part in deciding Pitt and Dundas, the Government of the day, to throw in their weight against them and accomplish the downfall of their monopoly in 1796.

So important is every part of the elaborate whole of East India Company politics, in the years when East India politics were never distinct from those of the country and the City, that it is valuable for the parliamentary history of the time as well as that of the history of commerce, to examine this 'shipping interest'. When the outlines of the position are made clear, the Braund papers serve a valuable purpose in giving a sample of its organization and personnel in the days before the struggle became really serious, and when it was still in the height of its power.

The shipping concerns of the East India Company had never been easy to handle. Nor is it simple to disentangle

---

[1] James Mill, *The History of British India*, iii. 355. Based on the Ninth Report from the Select Committee on the Administration of Justice in India, 1783 (*Parl. Reports*, vol. vi), p. 47 a.

[2] *Dangers and Disadvantages to the Public and East India Company from that Company building and navigating its own Ships*, London, 1778. (Guildhall Tracts, 308 (i) ; India Office Tract, 174.)

[3] *Considerations on the Necessity of Lowering the exorbitant Freight of Ships employed in the Service of the East India Company*, A. Brough, London, 1786, p. 32. (Guildhall Tracts, 308 (4).)

the development of the Company's shipping policy. The minutes of the Committee of Shipping,[1] which from the mid-seventeenth century dealt with questions of the hire of ships, have unfortunately been destroyed. The only records of the committee remaining are from 1780 onwards, printed by order of the Court of Proprietors among the general proceedings of the Company on matters of shipping.[2] The Court Books of the Court of Directors, however, remain, and they contain a great deal of important material throughout the whole period, and were always the sole source of evidence until 1698 when the Committee of Shipping seems to have begun to keep minutes.[3] From about 1770 onwards these records can be supplemented by the reports of the big parliamentary inquiries and by the various interchanges of pamphlet warfare of the last quarter of the eighteenth century. The best narrative of the growth of the East India shipping system is a tract, apparently unpublished, written in or shortly after 1796, of which a manuscript copy is preserved in the India Office Library.[4] It is obviously an official production based on the Company's records, the reasoned apology for the Company's destruction of its old shipping system, and is a work of learning and ability.

Even in the seventeenth century, when the basis of the Company's system of hiring ships was being laid, two determining factors of its future development were becoming apparent. In the first place there was already the danger

[1] The Committee of Shipping appears to have originated in a number of *ad hoc* committees chosen to deal with the taking up of ships and fixing of freights. The first mention of the committee by name occurs on 15 Sept. 1658 (*Cal. Court Minutes*, v. 284). There is then no further reference which would suggest a standing committee until 1660 when a question is referred to the 'Committees' (i.e. Directors) 'formerly appointed for the purpose' (*Cal. Court Minutes*, vi. 114). From that time on the committee appears to be a permanent institution.

[2] They were ordered to be printed by the Court of Proprietors, 31 Mar. 1791, and thereafter continued. They are here quoted throughout as *Printed Proceedings, Marine Miscellanies*, vols. 530–4.

[3] Ct. Bk. 37 a, f. 20 b. A resolution was passed that this and other committees were to keep minutes and submit reports to the Court, signed by the Chairman.

[4] India Office, Marine Miscellanies. I. *Brief historical Sketch of the Shipping Concerns of the East India Company.* This MS. has been used by F. C. Danvers, in the historical introduction to his *List of Marine Records of the late East India Company in the India Office*, London, 1896.

that the owners of ships hired by the Company would exert
undue influence over it. In the second place, already the
need was becoming apparent for continuity in the supply
of shipping and for a special type of ship to satisfy the
Company's requirements, needs which were the real cause
of so much that was undesirable and apparently unnecessary in the eighteenth-century shipping arrangements. For
the problem for the Company was the choice between open
competition and an organized supply of the shipping specially fitted for its needs. These alternatives are universal
problems, though in this case the fundamental considerations were strangely complicated by the facts which affected
every aspect of the Company's affairs, personal interests
which became vested, and all the results of the Company's
becoming a great semi-political institution where the worst
elements of eighteenth-century political life showed themselves.

When the Company embarked on its hire system in 1641,
the first ships were taken up for one voyage only, and indeed
there was never enough permanence in the earlier ' stocks '
to allow any other arrangement; [1] but when the permanent
joint stock was established, the conditions of the Company's
service could not allow this to continue. Ships began to
be built specially for them. In 1659 the Directors guaranteed to one Captain Millett, that if he and his friends built
them a suitable ship they would give her employment before
any other ship and on as good terms as possible.[2] Already
ships taken up for one voyage were generally taken up again,
and by 1668 it was recognized that they were hired for a
number of voyages, for the Company announced its intention of encouraging the building of ships specially suited to
its needs and promised that ships of 350 to 500 tons with
three decks should be given 20s. per ton extra ' for the
first two voyages '. Moreover, for the further encouragement of owners they declared that no three-decked ship
would be considered superannuated until it had done sixteen

---

[1] See W. R. Scott, *The Constitution and Finance of English, Scottish and Irish Joint
Stock Companies to 1720*, Cambridge, 1910–12, and the introductions to *Cal.
Court Minutes* by W. Foster.
[2] *Cal. Court Minutes*, v. 348–9.

years' service, and no two-decked ship until it had done fourteen.[1] Thus from an early date the needs of the Company seem to give a certain permanence to its shipping interest.

The pressure of personal influence and its effects were felt earlier, even before the freighting system was introduced. In 1601 the excuse was made to the Privy Council, for the slowness of the Company in sending out a venture planned, that it was feared the 'Committees' 'for some private respects' might be drawn to prefer ships not so serviceable as were convenient.[2] When the regular hiring of ships began the records leave no room for doubt that, as the eighteenth-century *Brief Historical Sketch* remarked, a section among the 'Committees', or Directors, soon established a predominance in the supply of shipping. The sketch asserts that they were in a position to do so because already a number of them were already owners of ships concerned in the reshipping of spices from England to France and Italy, and though no evidence is given for this statement it appears very probable.[3] The 'Committees' were the 'charter-party owners', whose importance and influence with the Company were causing the rise of the 'ship's husband'. It was not until 1709 that there was a revolt against their control, and the Directors were forbidden to take part in the Company's shipping. That even this prohibition was not thought to be successful is shown by the fact that the Act of 1793[4] laid down an oath to be taken by every Director swearing he had no interest in the Company's ships. That it was actually evaded without scruple is shown clearly by the Braund papers. During the eight years in which William Braund was on the Direction, he not only maintained the closest relations with the business of his brother the ship's husband, but remained himself part owner of four East Indiamen; and his was not the only case of the kind among his associates.

[1] *Cal. Court Minutes*, viii. 58.
[2] Ct. Bk. I, ff. 77–8, printed in *Cal. State Papers, Col. Series*, East India, &c., 1513–1616, No. 295, p. 129.
[3] I have found no trace in the pamphlet material of anything on which this statement might be based. It is possible it may have been a Company tradition.
[4] 33 Geo. III, c. 52.

Out of these two things, personal influence and the promise of the continuous employment of ships, there arose two rights characteristic of the East India shipping system of the future, permanence of 'bottom' and perpetuity of command. They were not even parallel rights, they were two aspects of the same right. These rights arose in two ways. They rose first from the position of the commander. When they came in this way they had their origin in the constitution of the tenders of ships. In the eighteenth century tenders of ships were made by three people, the ship's husband, another charter-party owner, and the commander, and the Company tried, apparently with success, to get in addition a full list of owners included in the tender.[1] In the seventeenth century they were generally made by the commander alone. This is important for the present purpose because the East India Company from an early date entered into particular relations with the commanders of the ships they hired and gave them a special position. In 1658 it was laid down that any master who wished to enter the service must be acceptable to the Company.[2] Thus, if the commander were himself husband he must be personally accepted by the Company; if one of the other owners were husband, he must submit the name of a commander of whom the Company approved for the ship which he controlled.[3] In this way a commander early began to be something almost in the nature of a Company's servant, as well as the servant of the owners, and this meant privileges as well as obligations. The Company felt responsible for his continuous employment. When his ship was worn out he and the rest of the owners began quite naturally to be given preference when they tendered another in her place. So in time it became the general practice for a commander to get both a ' permanent bottom '—or right to have a ship in the Company's service—for himself and the other owners and also the permanent command of the ship for himself. This command became in time a marketable commodity to be bought and sold like a commission in the army; in just the same way the ' bottom interest ' of the owners became

---

[1] Ct. Bk. 41, f. 9, 18 Sept. 1702 (United Trade).
[2] *Cal. Court Minutes,* v. 214.   [3] Ibid., p. 299.

a species of property to be bought and sold like an interest in a parliamentary borough.

The second way in which the rights of permanency in bottom and command arose was somewhat different, but the results were the same. It came through the personal influence of important owners. In one way or the other there gradually grew up that vested right in ships, the permanence of bottom, and by the side of it the vested right in the command, perpetuity of command. As early as the 'seventies the principle was established that no strangers should be employed whilst those who had already served the Company well were unemployed.[1] This principle included both commanders and other owners, in particular, of course, the rising class of ship's husbands, as has been said, frequently the commanders who had established their connexion with the Company, and then retired from sea.[2]

So long as the Company's shipping was extending permanence of bottom meant no more than a preference; the owners of the old ships had preference for the ships which they built to replace them. When it was stationary or declining, however, it meant that the bottoms with this preference enjoyed a close monopoly. The strength of this monopoly position was, moreover, recognized and used from a very early period, less at first to repel possible rivals than to keep up freight. It was inevitable that this monopoly should take form in some sort of organization. The *Brief Historical Sketch* holds that in the seventeenth century no form of organization was required, since the Committee of Shipping itself maintained the monopoly which a group

---

[1] The action of this principle 'may be seen from the careful rotation of ships which was by 1682 well established (see Ct. Bk. 33 *passim*).

[2] The following is an early illustration of the permanent bottom. In July 1684 (Ct. Bk. 34, f. 11) the *Berkeley Castle* was adjudged to be no longer fit for the Company's service 'being 15 years old and having brought home the Company's goods very much damaged'. In November 1685 (f. 154) the owners have built a new ship of the same name and ask for her to be re-employed. It was replied that she will be considered in her due course. After some further negotiations with her owners (who included in their numbers the Earl of Berkeley) the ship was taken up in April 1686 (f. 213) for a voyage to Sumatra. The first direct reference to permanence of bottom occurs in 1723 (not as the *Brief Historical Sketch* says in 1730) when in Ct. Bk. 50, f. 398, a new ship is tendered 'in the Room of the Marlborough'.

of Directors had seized.[1] The author appears to have exaggerated the degree to which the Court of Directors dele-
gated authority in shipping matters to this committee, but
not the power of Directors in the shipping interest. It
is significant that it is only after the Directors' power in
the shipping interest was challenged in 1709 that there
were signs of combination among the owners of ships
hired to the Company. In 1712 there was evidence of con-
certed agreement in the terms of ships' tenders,[2] and it is
soon clear that this agreement is the result of an organization outside the Company. Since by that time the position
of husband was fully developed, it took the form of a combination among the husbands of the permanent bottoms.
From 1713 to 1716 the Court Books show how important
they were becoming. These years saw a struggle of the
owners with the Court of Directors on the question of
freights, in which the owners submitted joint representations and showed other signs of co-ordination in their demands, and in 1716 the Court made a minute that it had
'Reason to believe That there was a Confederacy among
many of the Owners to impose the freight they demanded
on The Company'.[3]

When the Court thus complained of a 'Confederacy'
there can be no doubt that the organization of the shipowners was an accomplished fact. Every year henceforth
the combination controlled the tenders and negotiated with
the Court on them. That it was not only concerned with
charges for freight the future was to show more clearly.
Through its wide connexions the influence brought to bear
on the Company was very great. By these steps the shipping
interest was becoming a political power in the Company,
with a big voting strength in the Courts of Proprietors and
a strong interest in the Court of Directors.

The very circumstances which gave the owners this political importance were also a continual source of difficulty, and
it soon became evident that political importance was not
in every way favourable to commercial gain. Through the
great ramifications of influence of each ship's husband, every

---

[1] Cited *supra*, p. 91.   [2] Ct. Bk. 45, ff. 134 and 136.
[3] Ct. Bk. 47, f. 86, 8 Aug. 1716.

ship carried a number of votes at an election of Directors. Hence the position which made the shipowners politically so strong, when they acted as a body, tended to weaken their commercial strength by encouraging undue increase in the amount of shipping in the Company's service. The Directors, with their desire for patronage and support in elections, were always tempted to take up new ships which the trade did not require, and since the bottoms then became permanent, the evil was cumulative. As an opponent pointed out in 1791, there were always two interests within the shipping system pulling in different ways, however closely individual Directors might be bound to the shipping interest: the Directors who, for political reasons and the desire for patronage, wished to increase the numbers of ships hired by the Company; the owners who, both in the interest of their own close control and still more in the interest of the full and continuous employment of their ships, tried to restrain them.[1] Between the two stood the commanders of the Company's ships, and the Thames shipbuilders, who had the virtual monopoly of building them. They were closely allied with the owners' interests but entertained certain special interests of their own, obviously by no means always so hostile to expansion.

Thus the eighteenth century was, for the East Indian shipping interest, from the beginning, a continual struggle between political and commercial considerations, between the forces of expansion and contraction. As early as 1723[2] the Company had suffered a serious shipping glut,[3] and in 1726–7 refused to consider ten new ships. This crisis did much to crystallize out the claims and the organization of the owners.

The year 1751 was in many ways a landmark in this growth of owners' organization, and it makes a good vantage

---

[1] J. Fiott, *An Address to the Proprietors of East India Stock and to the Public containing a Narrative of the cases of the ships 'Tartor' and 'Hartwell', Late in the Company's service, with Remarks on the Conduct of the Company's Shipping Concerns, and the Partnership which the Public have in the Company's Profits*, London, 1791. (Brit. Mus. 1029 c 22/6 ; Bodleian, Godwin Pamph. 430 (1).)

[2] Ct. Bk. 50, f. 404, 7 Aug. 1723.

[3] Ibid. 52, f. 217, and f. 220 for the debates and resolutions of the Court of Directors on the glut.

point from which to survey the shipping interest in its full development. Its importance lies in the fact that in this year the owners gave the most convincing proof both of their power and of the solidarity of their organization. They decided that a large reduction in the number of the ships employed by the Company, a reduction from sixty-five to forty-eight, was essential to the prosperity of the owners. With this in view thirty-one ships' husbands, important and well-known men, second on the list of whom stands Samuel Braund, joined in signing an agreement,[1] the expenses of which were divided among the ships concerned.[2] This agreement, besides showing the unofficial power of the owners, throws considerable light on what a contemporary calls the 'doctrine of the permanent bottom'. The precedence of the recognized bottoms was already established; there remained for the owners the problem of reduction among the bottoms already in existence. It was decided there must be no destruction of bottoms, but a suspension, which was to take place whenever a commander died or retired on or after the fourth (and at that time the last) voyage of the ship, or retired after his return from it.[3] This regulation was to remain in force until such time as the number of ships was reduced to forty-eight. In the case of a need arising for the Company again to increase its shipping, the owners then pledged their united efforts to insure that the old 'bottoms' should first be employed. Thus the reduction would press as lightly as possible on both owners and commanders. This agreement, as the representatives of the owners told the Parliamentary Committee of Secrecy in 1773, was not formally presented to the Court of Directors, but was privately shown to and approved by some of its members,[4] and for more than ten

---

[1] This agreement may be found in full with signatures in the *5th Report of the Committee of Secrecy*, 1773, Appendix 8. *Reports from Committees of the House of Commons*, iv. 294–4.

[2] This is shown by Samuel Braund's accounts.

[3] This solution had been foreshadowed by a resolution of the Court of Directors in 1727. Ct. Bk. 52, f. 220. This resolution seems to have had little effect on the Company's shipping policy.

[4] *5th Report of the Committee of Secrecy*, loc. cit., p. 261. Evidence of Charles Raymond.

years the Company felt itself bound by a shipping policy in the framing of which it had no official part.[1]

The possession of a 'bottom' was therefore, by the time the East India shipping system was fully developed, essential for any share in it. It was an interest as well defined as that of an advowson and far more certain than that of most parliamentary boroughs. But it was also a complicated and curious one.

In the second half of the eighteenth century, when the agitated politics of the Company led to more rapid alternations of expansion and contraction than ever before, and when other dangers to the system began to appear, the development of the 'doctrine of the bottom' became more elaborate. Although a recognized right, it could not be taken for granted; at the end of the four, or later six, voyages for which the ship was employed, the captain and husband had to ask for permission to rebuild,[2] and (as has been seen) in the case of a policy of reduction, the right to the bottom might be suspended or subjected to an elaborate system of rotation. While in earlier years the taking up of any ship by the Company automatically founded a permanent bottom, in the later years of the century, when the use of 'extra ships' was found to add convenient elasticity to the supply of shipping, the Company controlled this grant more closely, and it became customary for numbers of ships to be taken up under the express understanding that, while the ship itself should be employed for its four or six voyages, no grant of permanence of bottom accompanied this arrangement. In minor ways too the Company began to exert control over this privilege; in 1784, for instance, it was laid down that when a ship was tendered as its turn came it must be built within twelve months, or its bottom would lapse.[3]

[1] There are several references to the agreement among the owners in the Court Books (e.g. 26 June 1752, Ct. Bk. 65, f. 28, and 25 June 1755, Ct. Bk. 66, f. 441), and it is always spoken of as if binding on the Company. In 1763 a very similar scheme received definite confirmation by the directors. Ct. Bk. 71, f. 35, 7-9, 6 April 1723.

[2] See *A Master Mariner, being the Life and Adventures of Capt. R. W. Eastwick*, ed. H. Compton, 1891, p. 41. The Captain explaining the system in 1791 understood this thoroughly. Nothing, he said, was written on either side, but the tenders were purely a matter of form.

[3] *Printed Proceedings, Marine Miscellanies, fol.* 533, p. 192. 19 Oct. 1784.

But none of these minor limitations seriously attacked the right in itself, and it required the pressure of a great party in the Company, backed by the Government, to overthrow this curious and characteristic piece of property. For property it was, just as a borough might be, but it differed from the borough in that it was necessarily a shared property. There were two intertwined rights within each bottom, that of the husband, representing the owners, and that of the commander. The claim to perpetuity of command, on the one hand, and permanence of bottom, on the other, were, as has been shown, complementary, and the bottom interest depended on both of them. Thus, while in the times of strict limitation of tonnage the commander must wait for employment until there came the turn in rotation of the bottom with which he was associated, on the other hand, the most equitable way of cutting down the number of ships was thought to be the suspension of a bottom on the death of the commander, the Company guarding the commanders against arbitrary dismissal by the owners. The ships' husbands and the commanders are therefore the first factors of the situation to be examined in order to understand the working of the East India shipping system in the mid-eighteenth century.

The permanent organization of owners which had obtained so strong a control over the Company that it could itself decide to limit the amount of its shipping, was no vague body, composed of the owners in general, but a comparatively small number of ships' husbands, a small, closely interrelated and powerful class capable of excluding rivals on the one hand, and coercing the Company on the other. The thirty-one husbands who signed the agreement of 1751, and among whose names was Samuel Braund's, include among their number men notable in London finance, like Francis Salvador,[1] prominent at Lloyd's, like Nicholas Crisp,[2] and merchants like Manning Lethieullier,[3] and ship-builders of the Thames, like Abraham Wells.[4]

---

[1] Francis Salvador. See Appendix IV.   [2] Nicholas Crisp. See Appendix IV.
[3] Manning Lethieullier, Turkey merchant.
[4] A. Wells. For him see *Chronicles of Blackwall Yard*, H. Green and R. Wigram, London, 1881.

Many of them were men whose names were to recur again and again in the representations of the shipping interest to the Company, and who had in their charge a number of ships. That they should claim to represent in all their actions the owners as a body, whom they began to call their 'constituents', was only to be expected from their dominant position.

The exact form of this organization of managing-owners is not so easy to determine at this time as some twenty years later, when it was involved in a struggle for existence, but it appears to have undergone no real change in the intervening years. In the 'eighties and 'nineties their opponents spoke of them as the 'club' or Society of Old Owners[1] (in contradistinction to their rivals, the new owners). They had their chairman and their deputy chair and secretary, and they kept up a permanent activity. They made every year their joint tender of ships; they negotiated with the Company whenever questions arose, such as a change in the terms of the charter-party, they formed a centre for more sectional representations to the Company, as when the husbands of ships taken up in a certain year conceived they had some special interest to maintain. Even when an irate ship's captain entered into legal proceedings against one of their number, he notified them as a body before doing so, and suggested that they might act as arbitrators.[2] Even the Government during the Napoleonic Wars, when their ships were required for transport, approached them directly as a body, only to be told that they considered themselves too closely connected with the Company to enter into negotiations with any outside body except through the Court of Directors.[3]

In numbers they were a fluctuating body. The thirty-one who signed the agreement of 1751 probably represented their full force, and on other occasions of importance they sometimes rose to about the same number. Ordinarily,

J. Fiott, op. cit.

[2] *The Ship's Husband, A-Narrative*, Capt. John Walsby, London, 1791 (in my possession).

[3] *Printed Proceedings, Marine Miscellanies*, vol. 531, Appendix, p. 959. 6 Feb. 1795.

however, their representations to the Company tended to be signed by about eight to fourteen names, usually of the same persons, who formed the core of the organization, and these were all husbands of importance and represented many overlapping interests. When an important negotiation was to be carried on with the Company, sometimes a committee and sometimes a delegation was appointed, consisting usually of the chairman and deputy.[1] On one occasion at least, as a last resort, to show the support behind them, they called 'a very numerous and respectable meeting of Owners of East India Shipping '[2] at the London Tavern.

The nature of the organization differs little from that used by any commercial interest in that century, when the art of commercial agitation and informal co-operation was so highly developed, except in the closer oligarchy made possible by the specialized class of the husbands. Both in its membership and activities it was a narrower combination, with more cohesion, and more prepared for continuous action than, for instance, the Planters' or Merchants' Clubs which made up at various times the framework of the West India interest.[3]

The second factor in the situation was the East India captain, or commander, who, without the organization, shared in some degree the power of the husband. The monopoly given to a class of owners by permanence of bottom, was also given to a number of commanders by perpetuity of command, and by the growing control over their appointment and actions, which was making them more and more like Company servants. This permanence gave rise to a property and vested right in the command, out of which grew the custom of its purchase and sale. As early as 1702 the Company had tried to prevent the buying and selling of offices in the ships it hired, but the amendment of the prohibition in 1709 by a Court of Proprietors in such a way as to exclude the commanders showed the strength of their posi-

---

[1] Sometimes a third member was added to the delegation.
[2] *Printed Proceedings, Marine Miscellanies*, vol. 530, p. 281, and Appendix, p. 387, 21 June 1786.
[3] L. Penson, 'The West India Interest in London in the Eighteenth Century ', *E. H. R.*, xxxvi. 373, 1921.

tion even at that early date.[1] It was not until 1757 that the Company again explicitly forbade the selling of commands,[2] a year after it established new rules for its commanders which marked an important step in the growth of close relations between the Company and the commanders of the ships which it hired. The prohibition was evaded without disguise, and only in two cases, that of Captain Collins in 1760 and that of Captain Tod in 1771 (and in the latter one may suspect that party reasons had weight), did the Company try to enforce it.[3] For by this time it was clear here, as elsewhere in the East India Company, that the question had become complex and bound up with wealth. The position of the East India commander, through his rights of private trade and his opportunities for smuggling, was a very lucrative one.[4] To purchase such a position a commander must be a man of capital and influence, though it seems that part of the purchase money was often raised on credit by ruinous respondentia bonds.[5] It is significant that many of the men most important among the ship's husbands and in the politics of the Company had begun their connexion with it in the position of commanders of its ships. Not only was £5,000 quite commonly paid for a command, and larger sums up to £10,000[6] were not unknown in the last quarter of the century, but in addition the commander had to have some influence with a husband to obtain a command at all. The commanders were thus a strong and important body of men, and, although they had no organization comparable to that of the husbands, they were capable of combining when their interests were attacked, and they had personal relations which gave them cohesion. One important centre

[1] Ct. Bk. 43, ff. 697 and 776.   [2] Ibid 67, f. 379, 3 June 1757.
[3] Ibid. 69, f. 270; 80, ff. 352 and 394.
[4] Captain Eastwick, who thought in 1791 of entering the East India service, calculated that, in a voyage of fourteen to eighteen months a prudent commander should gain £4,000-£5,000, but that the profit might be as low as £2,000 or as high as £12,000 (*A Master Mariner, ut supra*, p. 44).
[5] *Marine Miscellanies*. I. Private memorandum by a Director for the use of Lord Castlereagh, thought according to its endorsement to be by Jacob Bosanquet. This attribution appears, however, improbable, as the attitude of the writer is diametrically opposed to that which Bosanquet expressed in his dissent in 1796 (*Printed Proceedings, Marine Miscellanies*, vol. 531, p. 1003 seq.).
[6] *Letter to the Hon. the Board of Controul for India Affairs* . . . , 1803, p. 9 (Bodleian, Godwin Pamph. 1209 (8)).

was Trinity House, which, wielding considerable patronage and having close relations with the Government of the day, undoubtedly played a considerable part in the politics of the shipping world, though one which has not yet been in any degree elucidated. For this purpose all that can be said is that the East India commanders and ships' husbands who had earlier been commanders formed an influential element among the Elder Brothers, and that there was considerable intrigue among them for election to that dignity. The most notable example among them was Robert Preston, husband in the 'eighties to ten East Indiamen, whose influence was said to be all-powerful at Trinity House, where he was an Elder Brother from 1781 and the Deputy-Master from 1795 to 1803.[1]

The East Indian commander could sell his command, both because it was valuable and because there was no other way of reaching a command except through one of the limited number of ships on a permanent bottom. In other ways his position was not very different from that of the ordinary masters of his time. Indeed in some ways the latter enjoyed more independence, for there was no oligarchy of ships' husbands to control them. In the *Braganza*, a merchantman trading to Portugal, in which William Braund had interests, the master, Captain Lyons, was still his own husband, receiving the contributions of the other owners and paying out the dividends. The peculiar position in the East India Company is shown by the various relations in which the husband and commander, always different persons with distinct powers, could stand to one another. There were three main ways in which the power in a bottom could be divided.

(*a*) In the first place the ship's husband could have almost complete control, and be the sole *entrepreneur*. In this case he would bring together capitalists to build on an

---

[1] Robert Preston, created a baronet in 1798, whose portrait may be seen in Trinity House, London, is alleged to be the founder of the ministerial Fish dinners at Greenwich, though in his time they took place at his cottage at Dagenham Lake. George Rose, Secretary to the Treasury and an Elder Brother, was often his guest, and is said to have brought first Pitt and then other Ministers. (W. H. Mayo, *The Trinity House, London, Past and Present*, London 1905.) See also for Trinity House, *The Trinity House of Deptford Stroud*, by C. R. B. Barrett, London, 1893.

old bottom, of which he had been accredited manager by the old owners, or, when the. Company's policy permitted this, to build on a new one. The command was then to be bought from these owners or from the commander of the last ship on that bottom, if he were still alive, with the consent of the owners (a provision which often meant, it was suggested, a payment to the husband to get his support, though this the organization of ships' husbands officially denied[1]). That this position was common is shown by *The Ship's Husband, a Narrative*, by Captain John Walsby,[2] which describes his trials in search of a command from 1785 to 1791. He had, he says, been for ten years master of a ship which he had built himself when a connexion of his, one Captain Rice, husband to the East Indiaman the *Dutton*, urged him to qualify for the position of her commander, and promised all his interest in his support. By that time it was necessary, in order to become a commander in the East India service, to have done at least one voyage as chief mate on an Indiaman, Walsby agreed to go out on the *Dutton* in this capacity, on the understanding that the commander was anxious to sell the command immediately after the voyage. After they returned, Captain Rice told him the command was open, if he would buy it from the commander, and warned him not to give too much as the latter had given 6,000 guineas for it 'but that under existing circumstances that sum was too much'. Walsby therefore began negotiations, but he was soon warned by friends that Captain Rice was giving attention to other interests which were pressing for the command, and he taxed him with it, demanding a definite agreement. The latter after some hesitation replied:

'I don't think, Jack, I can do it.'—I instantly demanded 'How so?' and asked him if he had not always declared that the appointment rested solely with him, and as positively also had pledged his word and honor that I should have the command. Captain Rice replied 'If I must tell you, I am so wound and bound up with Preston (meaning Mr. Preston the Ship's Husband) that by G—d I cannot do it.'

[1] *Printed Proceedings, Marine Miscellanies,* vol. 532, Appendix, p. 1099.
[2] A pamphlet published in 1791, in my possession.

It was suggested that he was dependent on Preston's support in his own election to the position of Elder Brother at Trinity House, and that Preston pushed the rival candidate for the command of the *Dutton*.

After that disappointment, Walsby's hopes turned to Robert Williams, who was husband of seven ships. Five thousand guineas was the sum usually paid for his ships, and it was agreed that on the return of a ship commanded by the husband's brother, Walsby should buy the command; but here again there was a more influential competitor, and when the unlucky Walsby urged him to keep his word, Williams replied evasively by asking for the absurd sum of £20,000. At this point, after failing to arrange an arbitration through the society of husbands, Walsby had recourse to law, only to be defeated since the sale of commands was contrary to Company by-laws. His case shows how fierce was the competition for a command, and how strong in such cases was the position of the ship's husband, especially when he retained, as did a number of the greater husbands, a considerable portion of the shares in his own hands or those of men closely connected with him.[1]

(*b*) The second division of power was more even. Here commander and husband were both *entrepreneurs*. The husband might bring together some of the capitalists, and the captain the rest, or they might be relatives working closely together. This was to be found in several of the ships of which Samuel Braund was the husband, and one of the best of them, the *Boscawen*, was commanded by his nephew, Benjamin Braund. This division of power had considerable advantages, but it had also certain drawbacks, for it led to the growth of two distinct parties among the owners. This led to many quarrels about the rebuilding of ships on an old bottom, and sometimes the setting up of rival husbands by the hostile parties. Such a case was that between two prominent ships' husbands, John Durand and William Moffatt, who each claimed in 1788, with the backing of a party among the owners, that he had been

---

[1] *A Master Mariner*, op. cit., p. 42. As Captain Eastwick said: 'Thus the owners those East Indiamen had everything in their own hands, and the favour of any one of them was a fine thing to obtain.'

appointed husband of the *Duke of Grafton*. From the accompanying correspondence it is clear that there was a split between the old husband, Durand, and his supporters, and the commander and his party who had appointed Moffatt.[1]

(*c*) The third division of power appears to have become more important near the end of the century, when newer men were edging their way in, and bringing with them their enemies said, a more speculative element among the husbands.[2] Here the captain was the *entrepreneur* but the husband supplied the bottom. In this case the husband might merely possess that abstraction, the right of a bottom newly granted or purchased while in abeyance for the rotation, and he would keep in his own hands the management of the ship, while the captain played the part of *entrepreneur* and brought all the capital together. Such a position could only be found under the East India system, and general opinion was very hostile to it. In such a case the husband only retained the essential one-sixteenth share himself, while the commander and the group of capitalists, his friends, took over the rest. Under such circumstances the husband reserved very definite advantages to himself, and, as competition among the commanders grew increasingly severe, they rose considerably above those which accrued, directly at any rate, to the older type of husband. He reserved to himself control of the ship, sometimes an agency in the insurances of the owners' part shares, and often $2\frac{1}{2}$ per cent. commission on all expenditure passing through his hands, the beginning, it would seem, of the growth of the commission as against the fixed payment as remuneration for the husband. It was asserted by a hostile pamphleteer that this commission might rise to £1,800 on one voyage.[3] It is interesting to note that, while the husband was gaining increasingly large profits, and the commander was at any rate ready to pay larger sums for a command than ever before, the position of the owners by

---

[1] *Printed Proceedings, Marine Miscellanies*, vol. 530, p. 304, and Appendix, pp. 272 and 276.

[2] *Letter to the Hon. the Board of Controul for India Affairs*, op. cit., 1803, p. 17.

[3] See n. 2, p. 239. See Falconer's *Universal Dictionary of the Marine*, enlarged edition by Dr. W. Burney, 1815, under 'Ship's Husband', the first edition in which the position is explained.

the end of the century was very unsatisfactory. If one may judge from the case of William Braund, profits had never been for the owners consistently high, and as prices rose near the end of the century, and potential competition enabled the Company to resist each rise in freight, while the overhead charges of the husband increased, their position became very bad.[1] The pamphleteers of the shipping interest said by the 'nineties that only the friends of commanders who wished to help them invested their money in such a security at all.[2] This is an obvious exaggeration; even apart from direct gain there were many advantages which, for instance, tradesmen could most easily get, by being themselves owners of the ships whose stores they wished to supply. This is no doubt the explanation of the large numbers of purveyors of ships stores whose names are to be found among the owners of Braund's ships; but it is significant that by the end of the century it appears to have become general for a commander, when he had himself brought together his owners, to guarantee them 5 per cent. on their capital, a measure adopted, no doubt, to encourage the reluctant capitalist.

When the power was divided in this way, too, various forms of dispute could arise. A case which came before the Directors in 1793 was that of the dispute between John Fiott, one of the most active of the new husbands, and Samuel Bonham about the husbanding of the ship *Belvedere*. In this case Captain Greer was given the power to obtain a ship by some would-be owners in India, chief of whom was Sir John D'Oyley, a Company's servant. Greer approached Fiott, who had a bottom, and took over 15/16 in Sir John D'Oyley's name, 14/16 of which were then held from him by others, by a kind of sub-infeudation. When he took over the shares he promised that Fiott should keep in perpetuity the husbandship, as was presumably the custom in such cases. (The indenture, which is very interesting, is included

---

[1] It is stated in *Dangers and Disadvantages for the Public and East India Company from that Company building its own Ships*, 1778, op. cit., that 5 per cent. was the average profit. This seems to be, however, an unduly low estimate, made in the heat of controversy.

[2] *Letter to the Proprietors of East India Stock in behalf of the Present Owners of East Indian shipping. A proprietor*, London 1795. (Guildhall Tracts, 308 (11).)

in the correspondence.) A quarrel among the owners later arose, and Samuel Bonham was able to claim that he stood for 10/16 while D'Oyley and Fiott only stood for 2/16.[1] The court, however, felt incapable of taking any part in this complicated quarrel, which was no doubt of importance to a number of husbands at the time, and it is interesting to note that the legality of such an agreement remains an unsettled point of law.[2]

The commander and husband were then the two great protagonists in the curious game of 'bottoms' in the East India shipping system. The ship-builders, who built the East Indiamen, often themselves husbands and owners, also played an important part. They too had formed a close monopoly, which they enjoyed by prescriptive right and their close relations with the owners, as well as by their skill. Their names are those of the firms which became famous in the clipper days, for, as one of the most famous of them, Wells, said when the East India Company was in the 'seventies turning its face against bigger ships, 'I looked upon it as fettering the hand of genius; the East Indiamen are the only ships a builder has an opportunity of showing himself in.'[3] Barnard of Deptford, Wells, Perry,[4] Randall, Gray, and Brent, and later Wigram of Blackwall, were the recognized builders of East Indiamen, and were responsible (together with Gabriel Snodgrass the Company's able surveyor of shipping) for the development in the class of ship which so greatly improved conditions of trade in the last quarter of the century. There was throughout the century a steady rise in the size of East Indiamen which the Company itself, under the influence of vested interests, sometimes tried to check, but which it never permanently stopped. Under the enlightened advice of Gabriel Snodgrass, indeed,[5] it began from 1785 on to encourage the big

---

[1] *Printed Proceedings, Marine Miscellanies*, vol. 531, Appendix, p. 742 seq.

[2] Abbott, op. cit. Note by editors in 1902 edition.

[3] *Printed Proceedings, Marine Miscellanies*, vol. 530, Appendix, p. 133, A. Wells to R. Neave, written in October 1782.

[4] For Wells and Perry see *Chronicles of Blackwell Yard*, H. Green and R. Wigram, London, 1881.

[5] Gabriel Snodgrass was a disinterested and able servant of the Company. He had served his apprenticeship to Snell as builder's measurer in the King's dockyards, and became a working shipwright there. He then entered the East India Company's

ships of more than 1,200 tons,[1] which at first had met with opposition, but which the experience of foreign companies had shown to be more advantageous, at least in the China trade than the 800 tons favoured by the Company. In 1749 the three-deck ship was by no means the rule in the Company, but in 1758 the Company began to give them preference.[2] The coming of the copper bottom, first used in the Navy either in 1758 or 1762 but not widely employed either in naval or merchant services until the 'seventies, began to revolutionize both the length of life of the East Indiamen and its speed.[3] With the copper bottom it began to be realized that a ship was good first for five and then for six voyages instead of four.[4] On the other hand, the Thames builders did not always stand for progress. In the 'seventies and 'eighties it was shown that the threat of competition was sometimes valuable in stimulating their enterprise and bringing down building costs.

service and went as a shipwright to Bengal, where he superintended all the Company's shipping. (See his evidence before the Committee of the House of Commons to consider how His Majesty's Navy might be better supplied with Timber, 1771.) On 10 May 1758 he was appointed Surveyor of Shipping for the Company (Ct. Bk. 68, f. 31). He gave evidence and submitted schemes to two Committees of the House of Commons, and on other occasions addressed letters to the Admiralty. His *Letter to the Right Honourable Henry Dundas*, 1797, with appendices, was published at the Company's expense (*Printed Proceedings*). He did much to improve the type of East Indiaman, and insisted on iron ' knees ' as early as the American Revolution, while the Admiralty did not employ them until about the time of Trafalgar. (R. G. Albion, *Forests and Sea Power*, p. 393.) Albion, in his excellent book, makes the mistake of calling Snodgrass in 1786 the ' master builder for the East India Company ' (p. 77) and its ' chief constructor ' (p. 382). This shows a misapprehension of the Company's shipping system.

[1] *Printed Proceedings, Marine Miscellanies*, vol. 530, p. 196.

[2] This may be seen from the favourable comments on one of Samuel Braund's ships, the *Boscawen*, which was three-decked, in a pamphlet called *Journal or Narrative of the Boscawen's Voyage to Bombay in the East Indies, Benjamin Braund, Commander* . . . , London, 1751. (Bodleian, Godwin Pamph. 2070 (7) India Office Tract, 133.)

[3] The copper bottom must have been introduced among East Indiamen after 1771 and before 1786, as may be seen from the evidence of Snodgrass before the Commissioners of the Land Revenue 1791, quoted in his *Letter to the Right Honorable Henry Dundas*, 1797, p. 28, and a reference in the Court of Directors. (*Printed Proceedings, Marine Miscellanies*, vol. 530, p. 258.) In 1786 a motion that the Company should not take up ships with copper bottoms, as they were expensive and bad, was proposed but not put to the vote.

[4] The East India Company began to allow ships to do five to six voyages in 1788. (See the evidence of the ship-builder Wells and Mr. Hilhouse before the House of Commons, 1792. *House of Commons Journals, XLVII*, 1792, p. 312.)

How integral a part the ship-builders were in the established East India shipping system, was scarcely clear until it was challenged. Then, on the one hand, the shipping interest as a whole tried to exclude outport building in support of the Thames builders, and on the other, the Thames builders agreed among themselves in support of the old owners, to refuse to build for any would-be interlopers into their monopoly.[1]

Thus was the East India shipping interest as fully developed at the half century, with its elaboration, its personal interconnexions, its monopoly faults, and its monopoly virtues. When pushed to defend itself in the period of struggle ahead it did so frankly on monopolist lines. It stood, it maintained, for harmony and property, against a 'fluctuating fleet, fluctuating owners, and fluctuating captains'—all the reproach of a 'straggling and disordered trade' which seventeenth-century monopolist companies had thrown in their day too at free competition—and, in the days when competitive *laisser faire* had won almost every position, they still dared to maintain 'We know of no instance of a thoroughly good and efficient article furnished by competition or open contract'.[2]

They had, however, as monopolists, a losing fight before them. The restriction in the number of the Company's ships which they had brought about in 1751 was the last unchallenged triumph they were to enjoy, and they were to be forced into struggles both political and commercial. Scarcely ten years after their triumph they were first thrown into the whirl of party politics in which the Company became involved by its conquests in India, and then were forced to face the growing hostility of the general shipping interest of both London and the outports, and to share with the Company in general the attacks of the outports and independent merchants against the Company's monopoly. These attacks were now reaching their climax after a growth of a century and a half. Samuel Braund died when the rumblings

[1] *Printed Proceedings, Marine Miscellanies*, vol. 530, pp. 277–84, and Appendix, p. 387 seq.

[2] 'Dissent' in the Court of Directors of Jacob Bosanquet and John Roberts, 26 Feb. 1796. *Printed Proceedings, Marine Miscellanies*, vol. 531, p. 1003.

of the storm could scarcely yet be heard; William lived to hear them grow very ominous, but he did not see the deluge.

II. *Shipping Affairs in the Braund Papers.*

As an illustration of East Indian shipping affairs, as of the Portuguese trade and of marine insurance, the Braund papers provide evidence of a rare and valuable kind. They give not only information which can be used for purposes of comparison, as it covers a long series of years (in the case of shipping from 1747 to 1773), but also the close detail that business accounts alone can provide, which lays bare the workings of an enterprise at any given moment. In this case, it is true, the detail is fully available only during the earlier part of the period, 1747 to 1760, where there are the almost complete ships' books of the husband Samuel Braund left among his brother's papers, no doubt on account of his executorship. After 1760, the year in which Samuel Braund suddenly retired from business, presumably through ill-health, to remain in retirement until his death in 1766, we have to rely on William's accounts alone, and it is obvious that the accounts of a part-owner of a ship are much less complete and interesting than those of its husband. They are, however, sufficient to supplement very usefully the fuller information of the preceding thirteen years, and, in addition, to supply us with important points of comparison between the shipping of the East India Company and that employed in the Portuguese trade.

The evidence of William Braund's papers is to be found in the books already used: his rough journal from 1741 to 1764 (with its gap from 1745 to 1749 inclusive), supplemented by his cash book, 1747–74: his fair journal in two volumes from 1758 to 1774: and his two ledgers, F and G, covering the years 1758–74. That of Samuel Braund's accounts is of much greater bulk. His books must, indeed, for convenience be considered under two heads; those which deal solely with the expenses of building and sailing the ships, whether kept by the husband himself or the commander or boatswain, which yield evidence bearing only on the technical problems involved ; and those which deal more directly with the problems of business organization. It is the books of the latter kind which will be used here. The former, it is true, have more superficial attraction.[1] They consist of the following:

1. Three books of tradesmen's bills.
   (a) *Grantham*, first voyage (1746).
   (b) *Grantham*, second voyage (1749).
   (c) *Boscawen*, first voyage (1749).
2. Two small books of river pay,[2] and a portion of a third.
   (a) *Boscawen*, Gravesend (1741).
   (b) *Grantham*   „   (1746)—incomplete.
   (c) *Grantham*   „   (1749).
3. Two books of commander's disbursements.
   (a) Captain Benjamin Braund (*Boscawen*), second voyage (1752).
   (b) Captain John Oliver (*Grantham*), second voyage (1749).
4. One book, boatswain and gunner's stores and expense.
   (*Boscawen*), second voyage (1753).
5. Two books, copies of charter-parties of all Samuel Braund's ships.
6. Loose papers; several building contracts, very detailed, with the two great firms of builders of Indiamen, John Perry & Co. and Stanton and Wells, and some portions of journals and correspondence from commanders.

A great deal of life pulses through the bald entries of these ships' books of Samuel Braund. Through them the whole career of an eighteenth-century East Indiaman can be traced. There is first the gathering together of the owners, who take over the property of the new ship on the old bottom. Some of them are the old owners, some of them new men brought together by the commander or husband for the purpose. They take up their shares in sixteenths or thirty-seconds, and a first call is made on their capital. On the strength of it the elaborate contract required is drawn up with the builder. Calls on the capital continue as the building goes on until every one has subscribed up to the sum estimated in the meeting to cover the expense. Should more be needed then or later, a further call can be made by a general meeting of the owners. Before the ship is

---

[1] There is a good deal of this kind of evidence in the Marine Records of the East India Company, preserved in the India Office Library. See F. C. Danvers, op. cit.

[2] i.e. disbursements for wages made while the ship was in the Thames. These were kept separate from the wages for the voyage.

finished the time at which the Company asks for tenders comes round, and the unfinished ship is tendered. As the whole supply of shipping is in the hands of the association of husbands, this is a pure formality. Every ship has her order in the rotation of the bottoms, tenders in due time, and is accepted. As the ship nears her completion, she goes first into wet dock, and then lies at moorings off Blackwall, where the Company's surveyor examines her and a great survey dinner is eaten. Next comes the bustle of preparations for sailing; the buying of stores, the laying in of gunpowder and nine pounders, payment for ship's papers, the elaborate formalities of the Company, and often arrangements for passengers. Then the commander, by Company regulations, attends the Court of Directors, in full uniform, and 'takes his Oath and leave of the Company', and the ship begins her slow progress down the Thames. Next comes the coaching and inn expenses of the husband, who drives down to Gravesend to see her off; the last minute needs of commanders met by bill of exchange, their problems with drunken sail-makers who must for the time be humoured, and with first mates who suddenly and inexplicably commit suicide. While they are at sea accounts come back by passing ships of the progress of the voyage, and of the other shorter trips on which they are sometimes sent on their arrival in India by the Company authorities there. Sometimes there are record voyages. Captain Benjamin Braund of the *Boscawen* had a most successful first trip out, and also, as he wrote, 'a great voyage to Trinidado'. Sometimes their experiences were grim enough. One letter, from the *Fort St. George*,[1] headed 'Captain Robert Burdett, Commander, went out Third Mate', speaks first of the death of the commander and then continues

'We sailed from hence (Fort St. David) November 1st and arrived at St. Augustine's bay [in Madagascar] the 16 January last with a Very sickley ships Company who continued so till the latter end of May. Our Extreem Weakness obliged us to stay at St. Augustine's bay till the 25 March when we Sailed for Tullear

---

[1] The *Fort St. George* was not under Samuel Braund's management. Possibly a copy of the letter was sent to him because of the assistance his ship the *Grantham* gave her.

Harbour [Tolia] where we got the Same day and continued so very sickley were obliged to stay there till the *Grantham* Captain Oliver arrived who spared us an officer and thirty Lascars and Some Stores which enabled us to sail June the 10th for Young Owl [a port at the mouth of the Youle, now called the Manarivo] and Mathalege the first of which we made no stay at but proceeded to the latter where we arrived June the 30th and proceeded thence July the 26th for this place with 115 slaves Men and Women for account of the Company. Arrived here the 7th September 1750 after having buried 22 men besides Captain Mortimore. . . . Our Ships Company having been very Mutinous during our Voyage to Madagascar, Commander Kisle takes 7 of the ringleaders.'

One of the ships under Samuel Braund's management, the *Warren*, had a disastrous first voyage. First an infectious fever broke out, of which the second and third mates died, and the first mate and doctor sickened; at Mohilla, where they decided in consequence to put in, 'a great many of the Ship's Company died as per List.' Then

'May 19th 1750 had soundings in Latt 18.35. N°. when a Violent Storm arose at NN°. W°. and increased to such a hurricane that between 9 and 10 in the morning all the Masts went by the Board. Nothing left but Bowsprit, at the same time had 5 ft 9 Inches Water in the hold and between 2 and 3 ft in the tweendecks, tho all the Hatches was well Secured, had much to do to keep her above water, being obliged to have all the Pumps at work and could not gain on her till 12 o'clock at night, the Sea running exceeding high and the wind veering to the S°.W°. and not being able to get Jury masts we lay too [sic] 3 days and was drove in the open Sea a Violent hard Gale which obliged me to heave 19 Guns over Board all 9 pounders to prevent foundering.'

From India they report the state of the market, the safety of the seas, and express their hope that they will not be forced by delay to 'miss their passage' (the monsoon). Then there is the return at least eighteen months after the departure, the purser or a midshipman coming overland with dispatches, the ship creeping slowly up the crowded reaches of the Thames, dealing with the Customs and the Company; finally the meeting of the Owners once more at a tavern, the declaration by the husband first of one or more interim dividends on the venture, then a final one, after which his accounts are checked and signed with their names.

This voyage is repeated thrice more, and then the 'reign' of the ship is over. Few East Indiamen were sold in England, for their size made them unsuitable for other services; a few were sold for the coastwise trade in India, and made their last voyage out there for the purpose, the greater number were broken up. The husband declared his final dividend on the sale, and the bottom lay quiescent until its turn in the rotation came round once more, and a new ship was built upon it.

Interesting as the evidence of life in an eighteenth-century Indiaman, of prices and wages, might be, it is not the side which concerns us here, and it is not the most important information which can be gained from these papers.[1] The books here used are those which illustrate particularly the duties of the ship's husband, the personnel of the owners, and the costs and profits of investment. It is through them that a sample can be taken of the shipping interest which has been described.

These books consist of:

1. Journal I. December 1746 to January 1753/4.
2. Journal II. January 1753/4 to September 1764. (There are few entries after the middle of 1760.)
3. Cash book. Covering the same period as Journals I and II.
4. Journal arranged under the heading of ships, with a balance for each at the end. December 1746 to September 1764.
5. Rough ledger for all ships, and bank account. September 1748 to July 1760.
6. Fair ledger. December 1746 to 1760, containing the accounts of the following ships only : *Grantham, Boscawen, Edgecote, Warren,* and *Suffolk.*
7. A few copies of instruments, bonds, &c., in a paper folder.

No reference to Samuel Braund has been found earlier than the opening of these books, which as the East India Company Court Books make certain, mark his first activities as an East Indian ships' husband. Except for his apprenticeship to a haberdasher in 1712, his early life is left in complete obscurity. Unlike many of his class he had never been a commander in the Company's service, and

---

[1] A study of this kind has been made of an East India interloper the *Mary Gallery* 1704–10. (*The Papers of Thomas Bowrey 1669–1713,* ed. R. C. Temple, Hakluyt Soc., Series ii, vol. 58, Part II *passim.*)

although his brother Benjamin had commanded an East Indiaman from 1723 until his death in 1740 he had not acted as husband to his ship. He may, it is true, have already been interested in East Indian shipping as a part-owner, for we have none of his private accounts; his brother William was already in 1742 a part-owner of one ship, the *Stafford* (of which Captain Robert Hudson was the husband). William and Samuel Braund might be thought to have a family interest in the East India shipping, for shortly after their venture began they built a ship for their nephew Benjamin, who succeeded his father in the career of East India commander. But they were by that time already well established, and their interests were already wider. Samuel Braund succeeded to the management of a number of the ships which had been under the control of two prominent husbands who had just died or retired, Captain Jonathan Collet and Captain Richard Gosfreight, both of whom had been Company commanders, and who worked for the most part together. He thus entered at once into the very centre of the powerful shipping system. Between 1747 and 1760 his accounts show that he was husband to seven ships, the *Edgecote*, the *Grantham*, the *Boscawen*, the *Durrington*, the *Suffolk*, the *Warren*, and the *Shaftesbury*, though his connexion with the last was very short. He thus stood, during the thirteen years of his career, among the husbands of note,[1] for in ten years 1760–70 there were only three husbands who managed more than seven ships and only three who managed as many. His connexions were, moreover, as will further be shown, of considerable importance, and when he retired his work was taken over by two of the three greatest husbands of the decade ahead, Captain Richard Crabb and Captain Charles Raymond, with both of whom he had long been in association. William Braund held shares in three of the ships under his brother's management, and had also during the years 1742–74 covered by his accounts shares in ten other East Indiamen, only two of which, the *Stafford* (mentioned above) and the *Ajax* (from 1758, Charles Raymond husband) he held while Samuel was still in business.

[1] The most important husband of his time was Thomas Hall.

Certain facts of general significance emerge from the examination of these ships. The first concern the ships themselves. Samuel's ships were all taken up at 498–9 tons, as had by then become customary; but they were presumably from 600 to 800 tons builders' measurement, for though the Company in 1751 tried to check the building of ships over 600 tons, they were not successful in carrying out their policy. Most of Samuel's ships were probably over 600 tons, certainly the *Boscawen*, which was in 1749 the largest East Indiaman afloat, one of the three-deck ships which the Company was trying to encourage.[1] Their commanders were men of importance both in the organization of the service (the most distinguished then and later was Richard Crabb, until 1750 commander of the *Durrington*) and in the exploits which made the East India Company marine the founder of many of the great traditions of the English merchant service. Armed with nine pounders from the foundries of the successors to the ironmaster Ambrose Crowley, in war generally sailing in convoy, and furnished when necessary with letters of marque, they were eminently capable of defence and even aggression in the privateering wars of the century. Captain William Wilson of the *Suffolk* together with two other Indiamen, the *Houghton* and the *Godolphin*, won some fame by defeating two French frigates in 1757 off the Cape of Good Hope. The Direction presented each ship with a reward of £2,000,[2] gave Captain Wilson the rank of Commodore and some plate. Later he won further note as the friend of Captain Cook, and when in command of the *William Pitt* discovered Pitt's Straits in 1759, whereby it was said he 'pointed out to admiring nations a new track to China founded on philosophical principles'.[3] Samuel Braund's ships had their share in the exploits of the privateering wars of the time; they

---

[1] *Journal or Narrative of the Boscawen's Voyage to Bombay . . .* , 1751, op. cit.
[2] Ct. Bk. 67, f. 507.
[3] Quoted by W. S. Lindsay, *History of Merchant Shipping and Ancient Commerce*, 4 vols., 1874, ii. 579–80, without reference. I have not succeeded in tracing the source. The Company presented him with 100 guineas and a medal (Ct. Bk. 69, f. 85) on which was engraved, among other things, 'Mercury as God of Commerce just alighted on a Rock in the Sea' who 'addresses himself to Neptune (sitting thereon) for Information'. (Ct. Bk. 72, f. 97.)

also shared in its casualties; in 1756 the *Grantham* was taken by the enemy, fortunately for her owners only on her fourth and last voyage. To the more permanent dangers of wind and rocks the Indiamen paid a heavier toll. No fewer than three of the thirteen Indiamen in which William Braund was interested were lost at sea during his life.

The second general point of interest that arises concerns the owners of the ships. An examination of the part-owners of these ships, ninety-two persons in all, of whom four remain unidentified, shows certain well-defined classes among them.[1] The first is made up of men connected in some way already with the Company. It includes the Company's commanders, men like Captain Thomas Crichton, Captain Benjamin Fisher, Captain Henry Hinde Pelly, who later became a husband, and John Misenor, commander and supercargo, and the commanders of the ships themselves; it also includes husbands of other ships, like Captain John Pelly; great holders of East India stock, like Sir Matthew Featherstonehaugh, who played so big a part in the splitting of stock to get votes for Clive in 1763, and Manning Lethieullier, the Turkey merchant. It also includes Company officials like Henry Crabb (after 1746 Henry Crabb Boulton), until 1752 the Company's Paymaster, and clerks of the Company like Ynyr Burges. Contrary to all regulations it even contains a number of Directors. William Braund himself must have been put on the Direction in 1745, when the Braund interest was forming, as what was called a 'shipping Director', for he appears to have no other obvious connexion with the Company's concerns. The other Directors among the owners are Sir William Baker, Henry Crabb Boulton, John Harrison, Richard Benyon (whose partner Dodding Braddyll was also a Director), Captain Robert Bootle, Miles Barne, Richard Chauncey, Henry Lascelles, Charles Cutts, Nicholas Linwood, and John Manship.[2] Edward Payne, another owner, was the brother and partner to a Director, John Payne.

---

[1] See Appendix V.

[2] Six of these were also members of Parliament, Sir William Baker, Henry Crabb Boulton, Richard Benyon, Miles Barne, Henry Lascelles, and Nicholas Linwood. Other members of Parliament among the owners were Sir John

The second class of owners is made up of men of a different type, though equally closely connected with the Company's affairs. These were the purveyors of ships' stores to the East Indiamen in whom they took a share. It was clearly an advantage to them to have shares in the ships they supplied. Sometimes they were quite small tradesmen, like Joseph Bird, sailmaker, and William Taylor, ships' chandler, and received their share in the ship instead of payment of their accounts. Sometimes, like Stanton and Wells, the ship builders, or the firm of John Crowley, ironmasters, they were men of wealth and great importance in the growth of eighteenth-century industrialism.[1]

A third, more heterogeneous class consists of merchants, bankers, and insurers who had no connexion with the Company's affairs, but who saw in it an investment which might be profitable, or of friends and relatives of the commanders and husbands who were led into the investment out of friendship. Among the former seem to have been bankers like Sir Edward Ironside and John Blachford, insurance brokers like Nicholas and Thomas Crisp and Nathaniel Fletcher, financiers like Francis Salvador. Among the latter were such little groups as the Bookeys supporting Captain Bookey of the *Shaftesbury*.

An examination of the group of owners as a whole shows the curious interconnexion of London commerce. There was in it none of the impersonality of a joint stock company ; sales of shares were few, and new owners from outside the group seldom appeared. The Braund group may be taken as an illustration. Samuel, William, and their nephew Benjamin form a centre of family and business connexions. Leonard Pead, the brother-in-law of Samuel and William, and John Harrison and Charles Harris, the husbands of their nieces, have shares in their ships. William's connexions in the Portuguese woollen trade are also there ; Thomas Burfoot, his packer, Linwood of Clermont and Lin-

Chapman, Charles Pole, Sir Matthew Featherstonehaugh, Richard Tonson, and Brice Fisher.

[1] The interest of the firm of Crowley in the East Indiamen, whose guns and iron fittings they supplied, may be compared to the interest taken up by Boulton and Watt in the Cornish tin mines which set up their machines. (E. Roll, *An Early Experiment in Industrial Organisation*, 1930, p. 88 seq.)

wood, the Portugal merchants, and Tilman Henckell, with whom he engaged in ventures in Portuguese shipping, and Brice Fisher, the Blackwell Hall factor, already mentioned, an associate of Linwood's, with whom he always maintained close connexions even after the latter had retired from active business. With Brice Fisher we encroach on another group. His interest in East India shipping arose not only indirectly through connexion with William Braund, but more directly. A relative of his nephew and partner Nicholas Pearse was captain of an East Indiaman, the old *Montague*, rebuilt as the *Edgecote*. Samuel Braund became its husband, and Brice Fisher on behalf of the commander brought together half the owners. Among those introduced by Brice Fisher into the group were possibly Linwood, certainly his other associate, Sir William Baker (who had another link with the shipping interest through a relative Captain Felix Baker, commander of the *Stafford*, of which William Braund was a part-owner), and the latter's father-in-law, Jacob Tonson, the bookseller. A similar group is that of which the Lascelles and Charles Pole formed a centre. With these close personal relations, and with names so important in London commerce among its members, it is easy to see how the shipping interest obtained its powerful position in the politics of the Company.

A third point of interest is that from these papers some estimate can be formed of the profits gained by the owners of East Indiamen, the class whose monopoly was so bitterly arraigned. From 1747 to 1760, when Samuel Braund was in business, the cost of a sixteenth part in an Indiaman varied from £500 to £750. The increase in the size of ships and their building costs is shown by the fact that by 1770 William Braund owned no sixteenth which cost less than £1,000. The investment was always a risky one, for total or partial loss had to be envisaged. Judging from these accounts, moreover, insurance only partially mitigated these risks. The prudent part-owner insured his share for the whole of each voyage, but, as premiums, particularly in war, were considerable, in no case was the insurance high enough for him to avoid loss on his capital. In the case of the three ships lost in which William had a share, his losses stood at

£375 5s. 3d., £297 9s. 6d. (here he held two-sixteenths), and £52 7s. On the other hand, however, the gains were sometimes great. By combining the accounts of Samuel and William some conclusions can be reached as to the expense and profit of a sixteenth part in the greater number of the ships with which they are concerned. They are expressed in the following tables :

I. *Ships under Samuel Braund's Management.*

Ship.	Cost per sixteenth.	Life.	Net profit.	Remarks.
Edgecote	£640 c. £160 insurance. £800	1746–63	c. £900	
Boscawen	£680 c. £160 insurance. £840	1748–67	c. £800	
Grantham	£750 c. £140 insurance. £890	1747–59	c. £100	Lost on fourth voyage.

II. *Ships in which William alone was interested, and whose voyages were completed before his death.*

Ship.	Cost per sixteenth.	Life.	Net profit.	Remarks.
Ajax	£ s. d. 869 17 0 120 9 0 insurance. 990 6 0	1758–60	£ s. d. 375 5 3 (*Loss.*)	Lost on first voyage.
Norfolk	950 0 0 267 5 6 insurance. 1,217 5 6	1760–72	591 8 5	
Lord Chatham	939 1 9 39 1 9 insurance. 978 3 6	1767–8	198 14 9 (*Loss.*)	Lost on first voyage.
Verelst	941 0 0 119 7 0 insurance. 1,060 7 0	1768–72	52 7 0 (*Loss.*)	Lost on second voyage.

III. *Ships in which William was concerned, sold on his death in 1773.*

Ship.	Cost per sixteenth.	Life.	Dividends already received.	Sale price.	Net profit.
	£ s. d.		£ s. d.	£	£ s. d.
Norfolk (rebuilt)	1,023 2 0 No insurance	1771–3	1st voyage, 580 0 0	750	316 18 0
Latham	991 7 0 130 1 0 insurance 1,121 8 0	1769–73	1st voyage, 465 14 0	665	8 6 0
Cole-brooke	1,072 15 11 66 0 6 insurance 1,138 16 5	1770–3	None	1,600	677 12 10 (Loss)
Granby	1,080 0 0 40 5 6 insurance 1,120 5 6	1769–73	1st voyage } 2nd voyage } 928 6 6	860	608 1 0
London	1,120 0 0 74 0 0 insurance 1,194 0 0	1770–1	1st voyage, 250 0 0	760	184 0 0 (Loss)

The figures are not, of course, sufficient to justify any general assertions. A man who held a sixteenth in the ships in division I would, in the years 1746–67, have more than doubled his capital (about £1,700). A man with the same share in all the ships of division III would between 1769–73 have gained on a capital of about £5,500 only about £770. A man who held a sixteenth in each ship in division II would have lost in the years 1758–72 about £90 on a capital of about £4,000. Apart from the accident, however, that the earlier ships were more fortunate than the later ones, for on the one hand these three ships were more fortunate than the others under Samuel Braund's management, and on the other William Braund had in the 'sixties a run of remarkably bad luck, there does seem some support for the complaint made by the owners in the second half of the century that the return on capital invested in shipping was lower than in the decade before. The losses on the ships sold by William Braund's executors on his death, it is true, reflect special circumstances, for in 1774 the recent limitation of shipping and the evidence of dislocation in the Company's affairs must have had their effects on the values of ships, but the pamphlets of the time complained that ships nearly always sold at a loss.[1]

The comparison between the position of owner in the East India Company shipping service and a more representative branch of English shipping, the Portuguese, which William Braund's papers allow us to make, shows the extraordinary divergence between the scale of the undertakings. The shares in these latter ships are smaller, the dividends lower though more regular, and are calculated annually instead of on the voyage, and the gain much less. There are three ships in William's accounts from which the comparison can be drawn. On one of these, the *Braganza*, our evidence is too incomplete to be of much use, but on the other two, the *Henrietta*, an ordinary cargo ship, and the *Hanover* packet, one of the regular Government packet ships sailing from Falmouth, there is more information. In the former a sixteenth cost £130 ; the first annual dividend was received in 1752, the last in 1763. They varied very little, fluctuating between £12 10s. and £18 15s. a year. Under ordinary circumstances the ship would, therefore, have brought in a reasonable profit during the eleven years of her life. Interruptions during the Seven Years War, however, stopped dividends for several years, and their sum total was in consequence only £102 10s., a loss of £27 10s. The *Hanover* packet (Clermont and Linwood, husbands) was a more ambitious venture from William's point of view, for he owned an eighth of her, paying £447 16s. 7d. for it. Perhaps for this reason he insured his interest in her by the year, though he had not insured his interest in the *Henrietta*. His dividends for the years in which she ' reigned ', from 1759 to 1763, when she was lost,[2] amounted to £610 7s. 5d., a net gain of about £163.

---

[1] *An Olio*, prepared and dressed on Board an East Indiaman. The Ingredients by the Directors, Husbands, Messrs Baring, Brough, Dalrymple and others, London. 1786 (India Office Tract, 214 (1)).

[2] The loss of the *Hanover* packet in 1763 with a consignment of bullion on board gave rise to a case important in eighteenth-century insurance law (*Da Costa* v. *Firth*, 4 Burr. 1966, 1766. B. R. English Reports, 98, pp. 24–5).

The final point of general interest in these papers is that they give certain illustrations of the position of the husband. In the correspondence between Samuel Braund and Captain Alphonsus Glover of the *Warren*, for instance, there is a good illustration of patronage difficulties. Glover appears to have been closely associated with one of the most important of the part-owners of Braund's ships, Richard Chauncey, Director and in 1750 and 1753 Chairman of the Company. On a sudden need of a second mate when the husband was out of town, he accepted a nominee of Chauncey's. Samuel Braund was annoyed by this irregular appointment, but Glover replied to his reproaches that

' I thought it would be agreeable to you that Mr. Chauncey should be served sooner than anybody else, and there was no time to be lost. I stopt at Blackheath at Mr. Wells [the ship-builder] and consulted with him who you are sensible is an Owner, he thought I did right to give him the offer, as I think every Owner of the Ship would do, knowing what a friend he has been to the Ship and Still able to be.' [1]

There are also copies of the instruments appointing the husband, and his bond, which seem worthy of being printed in full:

1. *Instrument appointing Husband.* (copy)

' We Whose Names are hereunto subscribed Partowners of the Good Ship or Vessell called the Grantham, where of Walter Willson is Commander Do here by Authorize Impower and Appoint Samuel Braund of London Merchant to be the sole Husband and Manager of all affairs relating to the said Ship during any Voyage or Voyages that shall be made by her, till it shall be otherwise ordered by the Majority of the partowners. And we do hereby Severally promise and Agree to Ratify and Confirm all and whatsoever the said Samuel Braund shall lawfully do or Cause to be done in or about the Premises by virtue of these presents. The Thirteenth Day of November in the year of our Lord One thousand Seven hundred and forty Six.'

Signed by the part-owners.

2. *The Husband's Bond.* (copy)

' Know all men by these presents that I Samuel Braund of London Merchant am held and firmly bound unto John Blachford

---

[1] The reference is to the compensation given to the *Warren* by the Court of Directors after the storm she encountered on her first voyage. See below, p. 155,

Esquire one of the Aldermen of the City of London and William Allix two of the owners of the Ship Durrington in the service of the East India Company on the behalf of themselves and the rest of the Owners of the Said Ship in the penal Sum of two thousand pounds of Lawful money of Great Britain to be paid unto the said John Blachford and William Allix or their certain Attorneys Executors Administrators or Assigns To which payment well and truly to be made I bind myself my heirs Executors and Administrators or Assigns and Every of them firmly by these presents Sealed with my Seal this Seventh day of March in the Twentieth Year of the Reign of our Sovereign Lord George the Second by the Grace of God of Great Britain France and Ireland King defender of the Faith etc. in the year of our Lord One thousand Seven hundred and forty six.

Whereas the Owners of the Said Ship Durrington have lately chosen and appointed the above bound Samuel Braund to be the Husband there of. Now the Condition of this Obligation is Such, that if the Above bounden Samuel Braund do and shall from time to time and at all times here after So long as he shall continue to be the husband of the Said Ship the Durrington, well truly Honestly, and faithfully act and demean Himself in All things, touching or Concerning his duty or Employment as Husband of the Said Ship and also if the Said Samuel Braund do and shall upon every reasonable request and notice in writing to him given or made by the Said Owners or the Major part of them give a just true and faithfull Account of all his receipts and payments, actings doings and proceedings, for or on account of the Said Ship as he is the Husband thereof And if the said Samuel Braund do and shall from time to time within two Calendar Months next after the Freight and demorage of the Said Ship shall be settled and Adjusted with the United Company of Merchants of England trading to the East Indies, well and truly Share, Divide and pay Such Money as After all just allowances shall be in his hands unto and amongst the Several persons above named or the Owners of the Said Ship for the time being in proportion to their several Shares or Interests in the Said Ship, when and as they Shall demand or require the Same, Then this Obligation to be void and of none effect. But if default shall be made in any of the premises aforesaid, Then to be and remain in full force and Virtue.'

Signature of witnesses.

This evidence which we can obtain from the Braund papers is limited, and there are many important aspects of the East India shipping system on which it does not touch, but it is, within its limits, very enlightening. Its significance lies in the fact that from this sample can be formed a fairly clear idea of the shipping interest as a whole in its elaborately co-ordinated monopoly of individual owners. One of its supporters wrote to the Directors during its last struggle:

' So large a capital, embarked by individuals in one concern without either legislative sanction or any security (or an interest beyond the good faith of the Company) naturally occasioned an association like other adventurers for mutual benefit and protection.' [1]

An opponent said it had ' progressively advanced to such a degree of power and greatness as is not to be paralleled by any other Unchartered Commercial Association '.[2]

---

[1] *Printed Proceedings. Marine Miscellanies*, vol. 531, p. 970. Letter from Joseph Cotton to the Court of Directors, on freights, 22 December 1795.
[2] *Brief Historical Sketch*, op. cit.

CONCLUSION

WILLIAM BRAUND'S activities suggest and illustrate certain aspects of the organization and development of the eighteenth-century commercial system. It is, for instance, indicative of the mobility which the merchant's position gave him that he was able to turn in 1756, without the least change in the methods or in the direction of his business, from his trade in exporting woollen goods to Portugal to a trade in importing bullion. It is also indicative of the growing strength and complexity of the institutions arising in London less to carry out commerce than to support and aid it, that he gradually left trade proper and in the later years of his life concentrated entirely on insurance and shipping.

The nature and working of these institutions can also be seen through the medium of his activities. They illustrate admirably the business carried out on the marine insurance market at Lloyd's, still unorganized, though already both a financial interest of weight in the City and an association held together by common interest and the dominating position of the brokers. It is a pity that, as Braund was no jobber, they perform no similar service for the contemporary stock exchange. His shipping concerns bring to light another organized interest, this time of a curiously close and powerful nature—the body of moneyed men under the leadership of the ships' husbands who supplied and controlled the shipping hired annually by the East India Company for its commerce.

Finally, even in his retirement Braund's actions are characteristic of those of the merchants of the time, for, when he settled up his affairs, he put his trust in none of the stocks and securities of the great commercial centre, but in the traditional security, the permanent wealth of the land.

The significance of William Braund's career lies, indeed, in its very mediocrity. It does no more than illustrate the working of that economic system based on the organization of commerce which Europe had been steadily evolving for centuries. It was a system (like the system of land tenure which grew up with it, but fell before it) at the same time inherently individual yet inherently associationist. Individualism within the framework of association is the keynote to the institutions of commercial capitalism. The association becomes less rigid, the individualism more pronounced, as trade passes from the gild merchant to the craft gilds, the regulated companies, and finally to conditions of *laisser faire* capitalism. At the same time the steady increase of its individualism was made possible only by the increasing specialization and diversity of its associational life. For this reason it may be claimed that the commercial organization of centuries found its fruition only in the eighteenth century when the financial system on which we still depend was, if not yet fully evolved, at least clearly marked out. When William Braund was born economic development had reached that state in which he was in one aspect alone the end of the system; in all others the means to that end. As a Portugal merchant he was the 'spring and centre of commerce', one of those for whom the whole system worked; as underwriter, ship-owner, and (to a far smaller degree) investor and subscriber to government loans, he was one of those whose function, increasingly specialized, was to prepare the way for the work of such merchants.

In all his work, moreover, his importance was no more than that he was one of the many who combined to 'make the market'—that activity characteristic of an advanced commercial society. If the eighteenth century is considered not so much in relation to the industrial developments ahead as to the older commercial system that had long been in existence, it may be seen to be the great period of aggregation into these markets, and of their elaboration in number and technique. The result of their development was that an anonymous strength was given to the mass of those composing the markets that they had never known before. Economically these classes, merchants, underwriters, jobbers, brokers, still only partially specialized, dominated processes scarcely yet touched by the challenge of the manufacturer; legally, by the quiet force of custom, they had found a place for merchant law within the common law; socially they were self-contained and self-dependent with their specifically bourgeois values; and politically they were giving a new content to the public opinion of England. And taken as individuals the mass consisted of a great many men doing the same things as, and bearing a great resemblance to, this representative merchant, William Braund.

APPENDIX I

The Accusations of Fraudulent Sales to the East India Company involving Brice Fisher and certain Wiltshire Clothiers, and, incidentally, William Braund, 1754–5.

(East India Court Book, 66, India Office)

THE following is an abstract from the minutes.

Fo. 153–4. 18 September 1754.

The minutes of a number of meetings of the Committee of Buying were read containing their proceedings on the reports of the Company's over-lookers of cloths on certain parcels of cloth sold to the Company for export. Resolved that gross fraud had been attempted by certain clothiers and factors on the Company, as all the parcels were below sample. By the minutes of the Committee of Buying of the 4th it appeared that Brice Fisher, Blackwell-Hall Factor, had asked to come before the Committee and explain his position. He stated that he had not seen the samples. Resolved that he should be asked to give the names of the clothiers with seven marks (specified) who had produced the offending pieces of cloth, 1900 in number. It was also ordered that the Committee of Buying should plan new regulations for the buying of cloths, and 'that the Lookers over do not pass any Cloth that weighs less than the sample piece'.

Fo. 158. 25 September 1754.

A letter was read in the Court from Brice Fisher in which he asked to be excused from naming the clothiers. He maintained that the clothiers could all exonerate themselves, and pointed out that he wished to prove such a fraud was not in his own interest, and that he hoped the Company would acquit him of the intention. The subject was referred to 9th October when [Fo. 173] there was a great debate on the case. During its course Henry Crabb Boulton,[1] a member of the Committee of Buying, later Paymaster of the Company, asserted 'that Mr. Chauncey[2] delivered to Mr. Rous a piece of paper marked W.P. 500—and Mr. Rous told Mr. Boulton

---

[1] For his connexions with the Braund shipping ventures see Appendix V. He was also connected with William Braund in his Portugal trade and in many other ways. See above *passim*.

[2] For his connexion with the Braund shipping ventures see Appendix V.

that Mr. Chauncey at the same time said, you must buy these 500 pieces'. Expert witnesses were summoned, and Brice Fisher, called in, was told that if he did not disclose the makers of the cloth he would be held responsible as a principal. He replied that to do so would greatly injure his business, and asked for a week in which to consider the demand. Agreed.

Fo. 183–4. 16 October 1754.

By this day, on which Brice Fisher was to reappear, his friends had made another effort to help him. William Braund, also on the Committee of Buying at the time of the alleged fraud, sent in a letter explaining what had happened there, and vindicating the over-lookers concerned. A party pushed for his evidence to be heard before Brice Fisher was called in, but was defeated. Fisher, called in, insisted on the innocence of the clothiers, refused once again to name them, and withdrew. William Braund was then heard, and William Wood, clerk of the Committee of Buying, was interrogated in his presence. Thomas Howett, over-looker, was also examined.

Fo. 187.

Next day, after hearing Thomas Burfoot, packer, another of the Fisher-Braund connexion, who gave evidence on behalf of the over-lookers, it was resolved that Brice Fisher should be held responsible as principal, and that all factors should be so held if they declined to discover their principal on application. Further inquiries into the woollens bought the previous year were ordered, involving two other firms of Blackwell-Hall Factors, Elliott and Misenor & Webb.

Fo. 289. 5 February 1755.

In the meantime Brice Fisher had submitted. A letter from him was read in the Court giving full particulars about the clothiers concerned, and stating that Samuel Whitmore and the three Sevills, clothiers, wished to be heard in their own defence. The demand was referred to the Committee of Buying.

Fo. 302. 19 February 1755.

A letter was read from Samuel Whitmore, asking to be heard as soon as possible, as he was keeping witnesses in town at great expense. The consideration of this letter was postponed.

Fo. 308. 26 February 1755.

The Court examined a number of letters from Brice Fisher, containing evidence, and affidavits from Samuel Whitmore and his employees. The affidavits included that of a clothworker at Stroud, a weaver at Bisley, and a yarnwarper at Minchenhampton. All were referred to the Committee of Buying, to be brought before the Court the following Friday.

Fo. 311–14. 28 February 1755.

The Court examined letters from various persons to John Fisher, partner of Brice. After long debate the Court decided that it would henceforth accept no cloths made by Samuel Whitmore or the three Sevills, clothiers. It also began to investigate the cloths sent in by two other clothiers, Thomas Halliday and Randall of Chalford, whose names had been given by Brice Fisher. Misenor & Webb and Elliott were asked for the names of two other clothiers. A motion that Brice Fisher had been very negligent in not examining the cloths was put to the ballot after debate. The voting was exactly equal, and the motion was withdrawn.

Fo. 314. 5 March 1755.

The Court considered objections raised to the prohibition of purchases from certain clothiers, but confirmed its resolutions.

Fo. 327. 14 March 1755.

The clothiers Halliday, Randall, and another not hitherto mentioned, Davis, defended themselves by affidavits from their workmen. They were referred to the Committee of Buying.

Fo. 331. 19 March 1755.

Deverill, the clothier whose name was sent in by Elliott, defended himself in the same way, and was referred to the above Committee.

Fo. 339–40. 26 March 1755.

In spite of their efforts, however, it was resolved that no cloth made by any of them should be bought in the future by the Company.

Fo. 450–1. 9 July 1755.

On report from the Committee of Buying the Court laid down new regulations for the tender of cloths by Blackwell-Hall Factors. Each was in the future to give the names of the clothiers if called on by the Committee of Buying, and to certify that he had compared the cloths with the samples. They were to state further that, to the best of their belief, the cloths were not made by any of the prohibited clothiers. The weight demanded of cloths by the Company was to remain unchanged. Any factor found abetting evasion of these regulations would be disqualified from tendering for ever.

Fo. 509–10. 10 September 1755.

The decision must have been a heavy blow to the clothiers, for they are found here petitioning the Committee of Correspondence to allow them to send to the East Indies, as private merchants, the large stocks of cloth which they have left on hand. They ask that the reply shall be sent through Brice Fisher. The Court refused the petition.

Brice Fisher's name had previously appeared in the Court Books as the recipient of large sums in payment for cloths. Henceforth it does not appear. Neither Chauncey nor William Braund stood for re-election to the Direction of the Company the following year or ever again. Finally, among Braund's papers is found a newspaper cutting which runs as follows :

'Whereas an Advertisement addressed to the Proprietors of East India Stock, appeared in the Gazetteer, on Wednesday April 2nd : I hereby promise a Reward of Twenty Guineas to any Person who shall discover the Author of so malicious, so false, and so scandalous a libel. Lothbury, April 4th. 1755. Brice Fisher.'

So, apparently, the matter ended.[1]

---

[1] An undated copy of a representation from Brice Fisher to the Directors exists in the Newcastle Papers in the British Museum (Add. MS. 33055, ff. 84–5). It appears to be that referred to in the Minute of 25 September, for in it he tries to clear himself and the clothiers from the imputation of fraud, and expresses the hope he will not be expected to expose their names.

APPENDIX II

William Braund's Investments.

THE extent and nature of Braund's investments vary with the three stages of his life. Up to 1756, when he was an active Portugal woollen merchant, they were few. When he entered the field of finance, 1757–67, they began to increase, in particular the short-term securities essential for that occupation. When he was winding up his business, 1767–74, he sold out again all but the safest. He died with no securities but Bank and Sun Fire stock. His capital was then disposed as follows : £3,990 was still invested in East India shipping : he had the nominal value of £5,900 in Bank and Sun Fire stock, the market value of which, together with accumulated interest, he estimated at £9,111 5s. : he had bond debts, due from men with whom he had close business relations, to the value of £10,290, and £19,700 in landed property. Throughout his life he had invested more in bond debts from merchants he knew than in any public security.

Government Securities.

Braund held at various times shares in the Consolidated 3 per cent. annuities, the ruling stock on the market, and in the Consolidated 4 per cent. annuities created in 1760. In the latter he bought in 1762 £4,000 stock and in 1764 another £4,000, of which he sold £4,000 in 1768, £2,000 in 1770, and the last £2,000 in 1771. In the former he bought £1,000 stock in 1770, and sold it again in 1773, making a profit of £25 on the difference in price. There are also references in his early accounts to £400 invested in annuities which he does not distinguish, and in 1747 he put £1,200 into annuities, again not distinguished, for his sister Mary Branfill to transfer as the marriage portion of her daughter Charlotte. He occasionally purchased tickets in the government lotteries : two ten-pound tickets in that of 1743, three in that of 1748, and two in each of those of 1751 and 1755. As he never won a prize, he sold them later for a loss, for each ticket was also a purchase of an annuity.

In 1758 he also subscribed £3,000 to the government loan by annuities of that year, and £200 to the lottery attached to it. He sold his lottery tickets without completing his payment for them, but he completed the subscription to the annuities, and transferred the sum to his sister Mary Branfill in part payment for the estate of Gobions.

Until 1757 he sometimes dealt in the securities of the unfunded debt. He occasionally bought a few Victualling Bills, reselling them after a few months. The last of these, a bill for £315, he sold in 1757. He also held Salt Orders for £500 due for payment in 1745, but still unpaid when he sold them at a discount in 1748 after receiving interest on them since their payment had fallen due. In Navy Bills he carried on a steady trade in 1742–3. He bought them at a discount, to receive the full value for them on their expiry some months later, in one case at a great profit, as is shown by the following table of his purchases and sales:

	Bought.				Sold.		
	£	s.	d.		£	s.	d.
Jan. 1741/2 . .	842	7	5	June . . .	860	4	0
Jan. 1741/2 . .	482	14	3	July . .	490	14	0
July 1742 . . .	672	11	9	Sept. . .	(price not stated)		
Sept. 1742 . .	1,500	15	0	Dec. . . .	1,524	1	0
Jan. 1742/3 . .	463	10	4½	June . .	2,174	13	0
Feb. 1742/3 . .	594	16	2½				

Except when in 1757 he bought and sold one more of these bills he never seems to have invested in them again.

South Sea Company.

He bought South Sea stock only once, in 1753, when he bought £500 at 147¾ for £610 and lost, selling it a year later for £579 8s. Except for this he was interested only in South Sea Old Annuities. Of these he received in 1748 £1,000 stock worth £997 10s. from his sister Mary Branfill to repay in part her daughter's portion which Braund had paid down, and in 1761 he bought £1,041 for £815 17s. 8d. In 1767 he bought in all £2,000 stock for £1,744, reselling it at a higher price in 1768 and 1769, and gaining £42 on the difference of the price levels.

East India Company.

In 1742 he bought the £500 which qualified him to vote in the Company's General Court and, in 1744, when he was aiming at the Direction, he completed his qualifying £2,000. In 1755, when he was off the Direction, there was a heavy slump in East India stock; he sold out early but lost £243 17s. on his purchase price. He did not then even repurchase his £500 voting qualification until 1758, when he was able during the war to do so at the low price of 147½. In the speculative boom of 1766 he sold out at the great price of 277½, thereby gaining £355 18s. 6d. and wiping out his earlier loss. He never held the stock again.

More important to him than the stock were the East India bonds, the favourite short-term security of the market. In them he dealt steadily from 1762 to 1770. In 1762 he bought twenty for a total sum of £2,064 11s. 8d., and in 1763 five more. In October of the same year he sold them all, to buy again eight in 1765 and thirty-two in 1766, thirty of which he resold in the following year. He continued these transactions every year till the end of 1770, when he sold out altogether. They brought in interest, and by judicious buying and selling, a good profit on the different price levels.

Braund also subscribed to the issue of India Bonds in 1746. Under the heading 'India Bonds 5th April 1744' there is entered 'Paid 20 per cent. on my £2,000 stock, £400'. He also subscribed to the reduction of interest on the bonds in 1749.[1] He enters under the date 1 January 1749/50 'Received of the East India Company for premio of ½ per cent. on £11,000 for reducing the interest on their bonds, £55'.

Bank of England.

This stock, and that of the Sun Fire Office, proved in the end Braund's favourite. His earlier incomplete accounts show that in 1742 he bought £500, and in 1747 sold £1,200, to buy £1,000 again three months later. From 1758 to 1765 he held no bank stock, but in 1765 he bought £1,000 at 127¼ and in 1769 £500 at 116½. The whole £1,500 he sold a few months later, at a profit on the price levels of £299 8s. Between 1771 and 1774 he bought steadily, and he died with £4,000 bank stock to his account.

He also invested in Bank Circulation, the 'cover' taken up by the Bank in connexion with the circulation of Exchequer Bills. It was a popular investment, as only 10 per cent. of the subscriptions were paid down, the rest remaining on call, and 6½ per cent. was given on the first 10 per cent. Braund was lucky to get every year from 1750 to 1751 and 1757 to 1760 £3,000 in Bank Circulation, for which on each occasion he had only to pay his first deposit of £300. In 1751 he sold his subscription two months later for £304 17s. 6d.; on the others he seems to have left the same £300 in year after year, drawing his 6½ per cent. on it. He obtained the subscription through the bankers, Martin & Co. In 1760 the Bank appears to have ceased taking it up.

Sun Fire Office.

From 1751 until his death Braund kept fifty Sun Fire shares bought at £38 each to qualify him for his position of manager.

[1] The Directors had passed a resolution to subscribe to the reduction. See Ct. Bk. 63, f. 427.

APPENDIX III

Public Record Office. C. O. 388/47, ff. 15–16 (Board of Trade and Plantations, Commercial Series I.)

(Sent on by Henry Fox to the commissioners for Trade and Plantations with a covering letter 15 May 1756.) [1]

To the Right Honourable Henry Fox Esq. One of his Majesty's Principal Secretaries of State.

The humble Memorial of the underwritten Traders to Portugal, in behalf of themselves, and many others . . .

After returning their most hearty and unfeigned thanks for the favour done them in transmitting Mr. Castres and Mr. Consul Hay's last advices relative to the new Duty of £4 p. Cent^m imposed on all Goods imported into that Kingdom, Your Honour's Memorialists beg leave humbly to represent

That notwithstanding their great and heavy losses upon this calamitous occasion, (more than many could well bear) they are so much convinced of the necessity of re-establishing that Commerce for the Publick Welfare, that they are willing to submit to every reasonable proposal for so salutary an end; in such a manner that this Nation, which ought to be the most favour'd, may not, as hath often happen'd, remain still on a worse footing than their Neighbours, & thereby run the risque of losing the Consumption of more branches of the Woollen Manufactures than are already almost lost: In order to avert such an irreparable injury to the Nation your Honour's Memorialists think themselves bound to remonstrate with all due submission.

That the only View of the secret Article of the Treaty of 1654 confirm'd by the first Article of that of 1703, by these words, *As was Accustom'd*, was to ascertain and secure for ever, that British Manufactures should never pay more than £23 p. Cent^m upon the Valuation of the Tariffe then existing in Portugal : and in case of doubt about that Valuation, the introduction of New Fabricks or alterations in the Old, to be decided and valued with the Concurrence of two British Merchants, which of late years not being properly comply'd with, has occasion'd a great diminution in the expence of many Species of the British Woollen Manufactures, and an almost total loss of others : chiefly owing to a disproportion in the Tariffe between these,

---

[1] The complaints of the merchants are against the duties imposed by Portugal after the earthquake to rebuild the custom house, &c. See Shillington and Chapman, op. cit., p. 264. A Committee had been elected to deal with the merchants' grievances. See *Letter to the Merchants of the Portugal Committee, from a Lisbon Trader*, London, 1754 (Bodleian, Godwin Pamph. 1174 (13)).

and the Manufacturers of other Nations, who, besides having less to manage, have been more tenacious on all occasions in that respect.

When the Tariffe was made there was but few French or Dutch Woollen Manufactures that interfered with the British ; and those too of an inferior sort, which occasion'd a low valuation at that time being put upon them, and has continued ever since. But as they have gone on improving, so as to exceed the British in many kinds of Goods, and the Old Valuation still continuing on both, all their Stuffs taken on an Average pay only about £14 p. Cent^m on their real value, whereas the British pay about £19 p. Cent^m as plainly appears by the annext account ; So that this additional Duty of £4 p. Cent^m falling so much heavier in proportion will every day lessen the Consumption, and, of Consequence, the Exportation of the British Manufactures, especially of Shalloons, Long Ells, Crapes, Cloth Druggets, and Duroys, that actually pay already more than £23 p. Cent^m upon their real Value, on first Cost on board ; which has long occasion'd a Contraband Trade, often attended with great disgusts to both Courts, as well as hurting the fair Trader. Your Honour's Memorialists therefore humbly apprehend that this may be all remedied on proper representations, so as to put the British Fabricks on a footing with those of their Neighbours, by altering the Valuations of Some, and duely proportioning that of Others, more agreable to their real intrinsick Value. It farther appears by the annext account, and is notorious, that Hamburgh Linnens are valued so low by the Tariffe, that they never pay above 8 or 9 p. Cent^m upon their real Value, or prime Cost, and Britain importing few or no Linnens into Portugal at the time the Tariffe was made. These which have been imported since being valued at the discretion of the Custom House Officers without the Concurrence of British Merchants agreable to Treaty, often pay upwards of £23 p. Cent^m upon their prime Cost, which almost amounts to a prohibition : otherwise there might be a very great expence of white Irish Linnen, and still more of printed Linnens from Britain, if they paid no more in proportion than the Hamburgh Linnens do, in Portugal.

Mr. Consul Hay's Observation is very just, that those who made the Offer of the £4 p. Cent^m additional Duty had no right to do it ; for which many other reasons might be assign'd besides those he mentions. But as it has actually taken place ; Your Honour's Memorialists at least wish, that a certain time was fix'd for its duration, not longer than is necessary for the particular service it is design'd for : and that some foreign Merchants may be joyn'd in the management of the Fund, as was once proposed by the Court of Portugal in order to enlarge the Custom House Warehouses. The British Commerce is sufficiently loaded already in Portugal without this new Duty;

for by every £100 of British Manufactures exported from hence and consumed in the Brazils, the Revenue there receives £60 before the returns come back to this Nation; and the Portugueze Merchants can by no means supply their Colonies without British Credit and Capital.

The inconveniency of not having a Warehouse to lodge Goods in, as Mr. Consul Hay observes, may be great, but still greater to the Portugueze themselves, and especially to the Hamburghers & Dutch, who pay much less in proportion towards it, and make much more use of them than British Subjects, both for Import of their Linnens, and Export of the Sugars and raw Wool.

Your Honour's Memorialists must humbly beg leave farther to represent

That though the British Nation is the most favour'd in Portugal, by the letter of the Treaty, yet it is far from being actually so in many Cases; partly on the Score of Religion, from which others derive many resources, and partly by accident, for example, our Conservators interlocutory Sentences carry no execution 'till an appeal is determin'd, and most, if not all, the other Nations do, purely owing to the Nature of proceeding in the Tribunals, from whence they were originally derived, which will be a vast loss of British Property upon this melancholy occasion, by other seizing the deceased or broken Debtors Effects, whilst British Subjects are litigating Appeals, which some party or other can always be induced to carry on.

Your Honour's Memorialists therefore humbly apprehend this to be a very proper Juncture to remedy such a great Inconveniency, because the Court of Portugal is no ways interested in it farther than making a new regulation for the Scriveners; which, by proper Application, and the Assistance of the present British Conservator, a Man of Weight and Learning, may be easily done, without the least prejudice to any, for even other Nations would find it advantageous, to prevent their Common Debtors playing One against the Other, for their own private Interest, to the detriment of all their Creditors; Which with all the rest, we humbly beg leave to submit to your Honour's Serious Consideration and better Judgment, to give such Instructions to the British Envoy and Consul as may be most conducive to the Honour and Interest of the Nation, the Welfare of Trade in General, and the Commerce of Portugal in particular.

Signed.

William Mayne.	Fred. Standert.	Saml. Wilson Junr.
Godhard Hagen & Son.	Stephen Winthrop.	Richd Emmott.
Saml. Thatcher.	Richard Carter.	Jno Hyde.
John Steward.	Martin Kuyck Van Mierop.	Jno Townson & Co.
Ronjat Lehook.	Jos^h Mellish.	Thos Light.
Will. Baynes.	John Langton.	Thomas Gurnell.

Daniel Lambert.
Harry Thompson.
Thos Abr^a Ogier.
John Hookham.
Robert Lambe.
Richd Merry & Son.
Isaac Hughes.
Joshua Readshaw.
Joseph Gulston Senr.
Nich^s Linwood.
Steph. Thompson.
Thos Plumer.
Jeremy Freeman.
John Raymond.
John Mayne.

George Foley.
Robert Jones.
John Stephenson.
James Tierney.
Samuel Clarke.
Tho. Godfrey.
James Grosett.
Philip Jackson.
Arthur Stert.
Ja^s. Auriol.
Joseph Watkins.
Jno. Charlton.
Thomas Corner.
Jno Looge.
John Byde.

Tilman Henckell.
P. Wilkinson.
Will. Braund.
John Whitmore.
Joseph May.
Dan. Le Sueur.
Giles Vincent
Charles Thompson.
Willm L. Leyborne.
Thomas Theobald.
Willm Wood.
Chris. Roberts.
Ab^m. Hake.
Samuel Hoare.
Josiah Hardy.

Enclosed.

Comparison of the real Dutys paid in Portugal upon Hamburgh, French, and English Goods, being all rated to pay £23 p. Cent^m ad valorem on the Cost on board at the Port of Embarkation.

Hamburgh Goods.	Real Cost on Board.	Dutys Paid.
600 Narrow Bretenhas	620ψ530	39ψ376
500 Broad Bretenhas	664ψ481	42ψ409
445 Cres	317ψ600	34ψ082
112 Aniagems	690ψ809	66ψ845
1,200 Panicos	1176ψ900	141ψ324
200 Ruoes	969ψ300	77ψ740
100 Estopinhas	182ψ550	27ψ382
	4622ψ170	429ψ158

By which it is plain that the Hamburgh Goods do not pay much more than £9 p. Cent^m on the prime Cost.

French Goods.	Real Cost on Board.	Dutys Paid.
40 Camlets	600ψ030	84ψ026
20 Camlets, Scarlet	610ψ700	48ψ860
10 Sampareils [Sanspareils?]	64ψ300	11ψ212
8 Water'd Camlets	45ψ920	8ψ740
20 Wav'd Stuffs	56ψ000	9ψ108
16 Druggets	313ψ868	57ψ523
20 Galas	357ψ040	32ψ890
40 Sarges	813ψ409	155ψ020
12 Silk and Worsted Camlets	377ψ720	58ψ278
12 Barragans	148ψ120	16ψ560
	3384ψ107	482ψ217

By which it appears that French Goods pay little more than £14 p. Cent^m and these Articles are the Bulk of their Woollens, & all interfere greatly with our Stuff Fabricks, being much of the same Sorts, & serving the same purposes.

English Goods.	Prime Cost.	Dutys Paid.
48 Fine Camlets	576ψ360	103ψ040
48 Water'd Camlets	285ψ120	52ψ992
120 Narrow Tabbys	1291ψ875	201ψ664
40 Durances	263ψ272	49ψ680
100 Shalloons	599ψ257	164ψ910
100 Long Ells	502ψ272	115ψ000
12 Flower'd Camletees	79ψ312	13ψ248
30 Floretts	159ψ860	26ψ082
30 Callimancoes	213ψ833	. 49ψ680
80 Worsted Damasks	655ψ280	101ψ384
	4626ψ441	877ψ680

By which it is evident that English Goods of the same sorts as the French pay about £19 p. Cent^m and there are two Articles, viz. Crapes & Cloth Druggets, which pay much more; and the French have drove Us quite out of these Articles, tho' they had formerly a very great expence.

fol. 17 seq.

(Docketed ' to be sent to the Board of Trade with the Memorial'.)

To the Honourable Lord Hobart &
To the Honourable Horatio Walpole.[1]   Norw^{ch} May 6th. 1756.
Honourable Sirs,

As a petition from the Merchants in London will soon be presented to the Secretary of State to request his Influence that the Tarriff or Dutys of English Manufactury may not Exceed those laid on the French Exported to the port of Lisbon your recommending the Same to the Secretary will greatly Oblige S^{rs} your humble servants

Peter Colombine.	John and Joseph Gurney.
Jerem. Ives.	John Ives.
John Wood.	Edwd. Pearse.
Wm. Wiggett.	J. Churchman.
Rob Harvey	John Patteson.
Thos Harvey.	Isaac Marsh.
Wm Crowe.	

---

[1] The Parliamentary representatives of the borough of Norwich.

141

APPENDIX IV

INSURANCE BROKERS FOR WHOM WILLIAM BRAUND UNDERWROTE. *Total* 76

* Indicates a subscriber to New Lloyd's before 1800.   † Indicates one of the seventy-nine bondholders of New Lloyd's.

Name.	*Dates between which they occur in his books.*	*Information found in the London Directories, &c., 1738–83.*
Miles P. Andrews	1760–7	Budge Row (from East India Company Stock ledger), M.P. for Bewdley, 1800–14. Son of a drysalter of Watling Street. In firm of Pigou, Andrews & Wilkes: owned with F. Pigou the Dartford Powder Mills, and made a substantial fortune. A man of fashion, a friend of the second Lord Lyttelton (1744–79), and a minor playwright and poet. (Article by W. R. Dawson, *Lloyd's List and Shipping Gazette*, 7 Nov. 1930).*
Dick & Angerstein	1758, 1763–6	1738 Alexander Dick, merchant, Swithin's Lane; 1754 the same, Insurance office; 1757 Dick & Angerstein, Insurance office, Cowper's Court, Cornhill.¹ In 1768 the firm of Dick & Perrot is in the old office, and John Julius Angerstein †* remains in a new one in the same court. In 1778 the firm stands as Angerstein & Lewis, Throgmorton Street; 1783 Angerstein, Crokatt & Lewis, over the Exchange.
Henry Appleton	1762–7	1763 Insurance office, Throgmorton Street.*†

¹ This stage of John Julius Angerstein's business career appears to have been overlooked by those who have written of him.   See Wright and Fayle, op. cit., p. 115, n. 1.

Name.	Dates between which they occur in his books.	Information found in the London Directories, &c., 1738–83.
{Author & Campion	1763–6	(In the directories, Champion.) 1763 Insurance office, Old Broad Street; 1765 Austin Friars. The firm is not mentioned again. Author.*†
{J. Author	1769	
{Barclay & Whittle	1759–64	Never mentioned in partnership. 1738 D. Barclay, merchant, Cateaton Street; 1763 Either Insurance office, Tower Street, or D. Barclay, junior, Insurance office, Cateaton Street.*
{Brookes & Barclay (?)	1748	
Thomas Bell	1758, 1762–3, 1764–5	1744 of Mark Lane; 1754 Broker, same address.*†
William Bell	1758	1752 of Fetter Lane; 1754 Merchant, same address.*† W. & T. Bell; 1759 Insurance office, Change Alley.
Emmanuel P. Bize	1758, 1760–7	1763 E. P. Bize, Coleman Street; 1770 Old Broad Street; 1783 Cornhill.*
Samuel Bonham	1761–73	1738 Merchant, Ratcliffe Cross; 1749 Birchin Lane; 1754 Insurance office, Cornhill; 1759 Goodman's Fields.*
John Bradshaw	1762	1738 Broker, Fenchurch Street; 1749 Lime Street; 1759 John & James Bradshaw, brokers, Lombard Street; 1783 John Bradshaw, broker, Swithin's Lane.
D. Bravo	1741	1738 and 1740 only. Cullum Street at Mr. Salvador's.
D. Bureau	1765–9	1754 J. Bureau, Insurance office, Coleman Street; 1759 Bishopsgate Street; 1763 Cannon Street. D. Bureau.*
Butler & Mauger	1759–67	1759 Insurance office, Abchurch Lane. R. Butler.
E. Cahill	1759–65	1763 Threadneedle Street; 1767 Broker, same address.
Author & Campion		See under 'Author'.

Name	Years	Details
Hayes & Canham	1741, 1742	1738 Thomas & Henry Hayes, Insurance office, Cornhill.
Charles Child	1741, 1742, 1748–9, 1759–69	1744 Insurance office, Cornhill.
Henry Clarke	1764–9	1768 Insurance office, Change Alley.*
Fletcher & Cole (1763 Cole & Bingley)	1748–9, 1759–67	1738 Benjamin Cole, stockbroker, Change Alley; 1754 Fletcher & Cole,* Insurance office, Cornhill; 1763 Cole & Bingley, Insurance office, Exchange Alley; Fletcher, John & William, Insurance office, Cornhill.
J. Crichlowe	1741–2	1749 Lombard Street; 1752 Crichlowe & Staples, same address.
Thomas Crisp	1764	(Spelt Crispe.) 1763 Merchant, Tower Hill.
Robert Dallas (George & Robert Dallas in 1764)	1758, 1764–6	1757 Robert Dallas behind Royal Exchange; George Dallas, Castle Alley, Royal Exchange; 1759 Insurance office; 1763 G.* & R.*† Dallas, Insurance office, Castle Alley, Royal Exchange; 1768 R. Dallas, Exchange Alley.
George Dallas	1763–6 1764–6	
W. Deacon	1749, 1763–6	1766 Merchant, Cornhill.
F. Delon	1762–7	See under 'Angerstein'.
Dick & Angerstein		1754 Insurance office, Threadneedle Street.
R. Eastland (after May 1764 Eastland & Lewis, 1741–5 Wilson & Eastland)	1751–64 1764–9	1744 Wilson & Eastland, Throgmorton Street; 1757 R. Eastland, Insurance office, Cornhill; 1768 Eastland and Lewis, Cornhill.
Thomas Ellis	1762–5	1757 Broad Street; 1759 Merchant, same address; 1763 Savage Gardens; 1766 New Broad Street Buildings.
Jacob Espinoza	1741, 1759–66	1744 St. Mary Ax; 1749 New Broad Street Buildings; 1754 Insurer, same address; 1765 Throgmorton Street; 1766 New Broad Street Buildings.
Falconer & Farquar	1761–3	1744 D. Falconer, Budge Row; 1759 Falconer & Farquar,* merchants, Cornhill; 1766 Cannon Street.

Name.	Dates between which they occur in his books.	Information found in the London Directories, &c., 1738–83.
J. & W. Fletcher (N. Fletcher in 1741 and 1744?)	1760–7; 1741, 1744	1757 W. Fletcher, Cheapside (?); 1763 J. & W. Fletcher, Insurance office, Cornhill; 1738 N. Fletcher, merchant, Lombard Street; 1740 Birchin Lane; 1749 Lombard Street.
Fletcher & Cole		See under 'Cole'.
D. de Florez	1741, 1748	1738 Merchant, Camomile Street; 1749 St. Mary Ax.
R. Foxall	1766	1768 Merchant, Cheapside.
Abraham & Jacob Franco	1742	1738 Merchants, Fenchurch Street; 1759 Jacob,* Moses,* and Raphael Franco, same address.
A. M. Furtardo	1759	
S. Gardiner	1764–5	1752 Jonathan's Coffee-house; 1754 Stockbroker, same address; 1763 Threadneedle Street; 1770 Gardiner & Cancellor, stockbrokers, Cornhill (?). [He was a prominent jobber in East India Company Stock.]
J. Gay	1741, 1749	1738 Insurance office, Lombard Street, opposite Lloyd's Coffee-house.
Richard Glover [1]	1751, 1762–3	1740 Laurence Pountney Hill; 1749 Lombard Street; 1752 Change Alley; 1754 Insurance office, same address; 1763 Glover & Madockes, Insurance office, same address. M.P. Weymouth, 1761–8.
{ S. P. Godin { Godin, Guion & Co.	1741; 1750, 1759–70	1738 Merchant, Old Broad Street; 1752 Godin & Guion, Old Broad Street; 1754 Insurance office, same address; 1763 Merchants, same address. (The directories seem to have found the name very confusing.) Guyon.*

[1] This is 'Leonidas' Glover, the City poet.

Name	Dates	Details
J. Govan	1742, 1748	1744 Cannon Street; 1749 Islington.
E. Grace	1762–3	1770 Broker, Cornhill.
J. Gregory	1741	1738 J. Gregory, merchant, Eastcheap (?).
Godhard Hagen (junior)	1770–2	1774 G. Hagen, senior, merchant, Fenchurch Street; 1755 G. Hagen & Son, same address; 1763 Tower Lane.† (A prominent Portugal merchant and London Assurance [Director.] See under 'Canham'.
Hayes & Canham	1741	1738 Insurance office, Change Alley.
S. Haynes	1762	1763 J. Holloway, tobacco cooper (?).
J. Holloway	1741, 1747	1738 Insurance office, Change Alley.
Jonathan Hooper	1761–3	1757 John Ireland, Cornhill (?).
Ireland & Jones	1765–8	1759 Insurance office, behind the Royal Exchange; 1763 Change Alley; 1766 Cornhill.†*
Edward James		
R. King	1763–4	1744 Gracechurch Street; 1754 R. King, merchant, Mark Lane; 1759 Broker, same address.*
Laffose & Wilson	1765–7	[Lafosse.] 1738 J. Wilson, insurance office at the back of the Royal Exchange; 1744 W. Lafosse, Old Broad Street; 1759 W. Lafosse, jeweller, same address; 1766 Lafosse & Wilson, Insurance office, Old Broad Street.
N. Lynch	1741, 1749	1738 Insurer, Tokenhouse Yard; 1744 Cornhill; 1754 N. Lynch & Co., merchants, Fenchurch Street.
{R. Madan / Nicholson & Madan}	1741, 1759–67	1738 R. Maden [sic], broker, Lothbury; 1752 Hampstead; 1754 Insurance office, Castle Alley; 1763 Threadneedle Street; 1769 Nicholas Lane.
Abraham de Mattos	1762–5	Moses de Mattos was a broker in 1738, St. Mary Ax. Abraham first mentioned in 1763, broker, St. Mary Ax.
Isaac de Mattos	1758, 1764	Isaac, first mentioned in 1757, Fenchurch Street; 1759 Merchant, nr. Crutched Friars; 1766 Exchange Alley; 1783 Mark Lane.

3843·2

K

Name.	Dates between which they occur in his books.	Information found in the London directories, &c., 1738–83.
Butler & Mauger		*See under* 'Butler'.
Meyer & Staple	1772	1738 J. Meyer, merchant, Bucklersbury (?) or 1744 P. Meyer & Co., Austin Friars, or 1749 H. Meyer* at Mr. Bonham's Leadenhall Street (?). P. Stapel, merchant, Sherbourne Lane (?). J. Staple*; 1783 Meyer and Stepple [*sic*], insurance office, Nicholas Lane.
John Miller (?)	1741	
Andrew Moffat (after 1762, Andrew and John Moffat & Co.)	1750, 1759–74	1752 Lombard Street; 1754 Insurance office, same address; 1768 John Moffatt, Sun Fire Office Director, same address.
S. Nicholson	1741	
J. S. & J. Nokes	1751, 1759	1738 J. Nokes, merchant, Nicholas Lane; 1744 J. & P. Nokes, Exchange Alley; 1749 J. & G. Nokes, same address; 1754 Insurers, same address.
Gregory Olive	1762–70	1763 Merchant, opposite the Monument; 1767 Wine merchant, Garlick Hill; 1770 Cannon Street.*†
S. Onely	1741	1738 Merchant, Lawrence Pountney Lane.
John Page (Junior)	1764–8	1766 Insurance office, Cheapside; 1767 Page & Basin, insurance office, same address.
Moses da Paiba	1749, 1763–5	1744 St. Mary Ax.; 1757 Cornhill; 1759 Insurance office, same address.
Marmaduke & R. Peacock	1764	1752 M. Peacock, Coleman Street; 1754 Broker, Lombard Street; 1783 M.*† & R. Peacock,* brokers, Corn- [hill.
W. Reed	1741	1740 Merchant, Fenchurch Street.*

Name	Dates	Details
John & Travers Richards (later John Richards & Co.)	1741, 1759–63; 1764	1749 Change Alley; 1752 Insurance office; 1766 Richards & Hornbuckle, same address; 1767 John Richards* & John Manesty, insurance office, same address.
W. Salkeld	1741, 1749	1752 C. Salkeld, Ludgate Street (?).
F. Salvador	1742	1738 Merchant, Lime Street, financier acting with Joseph Salvador.
John Schiffner	1766–8	1744 Henry Shiffner, Bishopsgate Street; 1752 H. and J. Shiffner, merchants, Fenchurch Street; 1755 Old Broad Street.
Isaac Serra	1758, 1764–6	1744 Phineas Gomez Serra, Gun Yard, Houndsditch;
Phineas Serra	1741, 1749, 1759–86	1752 Phineas Serra, Fenchurch Street; 1754 Merchant, same address.
Manuel Francis Silva & Co.	1759–68	1749 Manuel Francis Silva of Bishopsgate Street; 1754 Merchant of Crutched Friars; 1757 St. Mary Ax.; 1759 & Son, same address.
D. Solomon	1749	1749 Houndsditch; 1754 Merchant, same address; 1757 Crutched Friars.
Roger Staple	1764	1749 Roger Staples, Basinghall Street; 1754 Tokenhouse Yard.
Meyer & Staple		See 'Meyer'.
G. Westgarth	1741	1740 Billingsgate.
Barclay & Whittle		See 'Barclay'.
Jacob Wilkinson	1758, 1764	1757 Abchurch Lane; 1759 Merchant, same address.*
Wilkinson & Rutherford	1765–7	M.P. for Berwick-on-Tweed, 1774–80. Director East India Company, 1782–5.
Samuel Williams	1759	1757 Gracechurch Street; 1759 Factor, same address; 1763 Threadneedle Street.*

K*

Name.	Dates between which they occur in his books.	Information found in the London directories, &c., 1738–83.
John Wilson	1741, 1762–4	1738 Insurance office behind Royal Exchange; 1763 Throgmorton Street; 1770 Old Broad Street; 1783* Old Bethlem.*†
Thomas Wilson	1759	1740 Turkey merchant and grain dyer, Bow; 1752 Garraway's Coffee-house; 1754 Broker, same address.*

MERCHANTS WHOSE POLICIES WILLIAM BRAUND UNDERWROTE. Total 15

Name.	Dates between which their names occur in W. Braund's accounts.	Information found in the London directories, &c., 1738–83.
F. Allwood	1760	
Barrington Buggin	1770	1744 St. Dunstan's Hill; 1749 Brewer's Key, Thames Street; 1754 Merchant, Crutched Friars;[1] 1767 Philpot Lane (an East India Company ships' husband, insures here two East Indiamen).
Samuel Chollett	1759	At first clerk, then partner of James Bourdieu. West India merchant, Lime Street. First mentioned in directories 1763, merchant at Mr. Bourdieu's.*†
William du Bois	1761–9	1754 Merchant, New Broad Street; 1783 Bishopsgate Street.

[1] He was the owner or lessee of a free wharf or quay. See petitions in Guildhall records. Journal of Common Council, 63, f. 238 b.

Name	Dates	Notes
J. Friedenburg	1764-6	1749 John Fridenburg, Ironmonger Lane; 1754 Warehouseman, same address; 1763 Fridenburg & Davis, same address.
Grubb & Watson	1761-3	1763 Merchants, Billiter Square. Brook Watson (?).*†
Abraham Hake	1761	1759 Merchant, New Broad Street; 1763 Cannon Street; 1768 Lombard Street, South Sea Director.
P. Harrison	1770-2	1767 Merchant, Throgmorton Street.
Captain Hayes	1764	1767 Captain J. Hays, Southwark; 1770 Merchant, same address.
Captain T. Hill	1765-6	1752 Captain Thomas Hill, Fenchurch Street; Royal Exchange Assurance Director, 1755.
George Hogsflesh	1765-9	Clerk insuring first for Sir William Baker, then for Samuel Baker.
Nouaille & Harrison	1765-9	1757 Nouaille & Harrison, Throgmorton Street; 1763 Nouaille Harrison & Bray, St. Mary Ax.; 1765 Nouaille and Harrison, St. Mary Ax.
Isaac Sumada	1760-3	Acting for D. Sumada.
Thomas Vigne	1755, 1759-60	1738 Merchant, Throgmorton Street; 1740 St. Mary Ax.; 1754 Threadneedle Street; 1757 Walbrook; 1759 Vigne & Chauncy, same address (see p. 13 above). (Braund's account continued in his widow's name from August 1761.)
Grubb & Watson		See under 'Grubb'.
George Wombwell, senior and junior	1764	1749 Wombwell & Grand, Crutched Friars; 1757 George Wombwell, same address; 1763 George Wombwell, senior & junior, same address. George Wombwell was in 1766-8 and 1773-83 Director of the East India Company. M.P. for Huntingdon 1774-80 and for Honiton 1780-6. He was made a baronet in 1780. Chairman of the East India Company 1777-8.

APPENDIX V

A list of the ships under the Management of Samuel Braund, with their owners, and the occupation of the owners.

The 'Edgecote'.

Built 'in the room of the *Montague*' by John Perry & Co. Commander, Captain John Pearse. Husband, until 1760 Samuel Braund, then Captain Richard Crabb. She went through her four voyages between 1749 and 1763 without disaster, declaring good dividends, until a heavy call of £384 per sixteenth on her fourth voyage, following an accident on her third,[1] decreased her value as an investment. The following is a list of her owners, a distinction being made between those brought together by Brice Fisher on behalf of the commander, and those whose names came in directly to the husband:

1. *Sent in by Brice Fisher.*

William Braund, Portugal merchant and insurer, Director of the East India Company.

Sir John Chapman, Bart., M.P. for Taunton 1741–8. Sheriff of Herts. Merchant and director of the South Sea Company.

Sold to

Charles Cutts, director of the East India Company.

Brice Fisher, M.P. for Malmesbury 1754–61; Boroughbridge 1761–8. Blackwell-Hall Factor.

Sold to

Sir William Baker, Kt., M.P. for Plympton Earl 1747–68. Alderman. Director of the East India Company, West India and America merchant.

Henry Fynes, Jeweller.

Tilman Henckell, merchant.

Nicholas Linwood, M.P. for Stockbridge 1761–8. Aldburgh 1768–73. Director of the East India Company, of Clermont and Linwood, Portugal wine merchants.

John Manship, director of the East India Company. Merchant.

[1] Ct. Bk. 67, f. 466. On 3 June 1757 the Committee of Private Trade was ordered by the Court of Directors to investigate the case of the *Edgecote*, which had been aground returning from Mocha and thrown overboard Company goods. On 1 February 1758 it was resolved that the *Edgecote* should pay for damaged coffee. Ct. Bk. 68, f. 259. 31 January 1759, Samuel Braund protested as he maintained the commander was not to blame. f. 279. 28 February 1759, the Directors credited the owners with £2,800 for the damaged goods.

Charles Pole, M.P. for Liverpool 1756–61. West India merchant and insurer.

Thomas Streatfield, linen-draper.

Jacob Tonson, bookseller. Brother-in-law of Sir William Baker.

2. *Received by Samuel Braund.*

Miles Barne. Miles Barne, Junior, M.P. for Dunwich 1741–54 and 1764–80. Miles Barne, Senior, had been in 1738 chief of one of the two Councils of Supercargoes of the East India Company at Canton[1] and in 1733 and 1736–9 a director of the Company, but the last year he became insane[2] and died in 1743.

Richard Boddicott, West India merchant and insurer.

Samuel Braund, ships' husband.

Richard Chauncey, director and chairman of the East India Company. Linen-draper, also of Chauncey and Vigne, gunpowder merchants (see above p. 13).

Henry Crabb (Boulton), M.P. for Worcester 1754–73. Paymaster to the East India Company until 1752. Director from 1753–73. Several times Chairman.

Sir Matthew Featherstonehaugh, M.P. for Morpeth 1755–61. Portsmouth 1761–74. A great holder of East India stock.

William Partridge, Blackwell-Hall Factor.

John Small, merchant and Insurer.

Richard Tonson, M.P. for Wallingford 1747–54; New Windsor 1768–72. Bookseller. Partner and brother of Jacob Tonson above.

The 'Grantham'.

It does not appear by whom she was built. Launched 1745. Commander, Captain Walter Wilson until his death at sea in 1750, then Captain John Oliver. Husband, Samuel Braund. She went through three voyages without misadventure, but was taken in 1756 on her fourth by the French. The following is a list of her owners:

Joseph Bird, Sail-maker.

D. Bisson, distiller.

Samuel Braund, ships' husband.

William Braund, director of the East India Company. Portugal merchant and insurer.

Charles Carne of Paddington, gent. Of Carne and Ellison, linen-drapers (?).

John Chase, of Chase and Harvey, linen-drapers (?).

[1] H. B. Morse, *The East India Company Trading to China*, vol. i, p. 265.
[2] Ct. Bk. 59, f. 163.

Captain Jonathan Collet, ships' husband. Late Company's commander. d. 1746. Royal Exchange Assurance Director.

Captain Crichton, Company's commander.

John Debonnaire, merchant. East India Company Director. d. c. 1747.

Thomas Grainger, appears to have been closely connected with John Thomlinson. See below.

Captain Richard Gosfreight, ships' husband. Late Company's commander. d. c. 1746.

Sold to

Captain Robert Brooke, Company's commander.

H. Hinde, biscuit dealer. 1761 himself a ships' husband.

Henry Lascelles, M.P. for Northallerton 1745–84. Director of the East India Company. West India merchant.

Captain Henry Lascelles, Company's commander.

Charles Pole, M.P. for Liverpool 1756–61. West India merchant and insurer.

John Sheron, cooper.

Jeremiah Smith, merchant. He sold shot and ' Holland Duck ' to Samuel Braund.

William Taylor, ship chandler.

Captain John Thomlinson, West India planter and merchant. Father of John Thomlinson, America merchant, his executor.[1]

The ' Boscawen '.

Built by Perry & Co. Commander, Captain Benjamin Braund. Husband, Samuel Braund until 1760, then Captain Richard Crabb. She did her four voyages from 1748 and onwards. Her first two brought in only fair dividends, and there is reference to a lawsuit to assess damages in a collision with the *Levant Galley*. An average was also obtained from her insurers on her fourth voyage, which was, however, unusually successful, bringing in a dividend of £550 per sixteenth. The following is a list of her owners :

Sir William Baker, Kt., M.P. for Plymton Earl 1747–68. Alderman. Director of the East India Company. West India and America merchant.

Samuel Braund, ships' husband.

William Braund, director of the East India Company. Portugal merchant and insurer.

H. Crabb (Boulton), M.P. for Worcester 1754–73. Paymaster to the East India Company until 1752. Director from 1753 to 1773. Several times Chairman.

---

[1] See L. B. Namier, *England in the Age of the American Revolution*, pp. 286–7.

Charles Child, merchant and insurance broker.

Ambrose & John Crowley, ironmasters, successors of Sir Ambrose Crowley.

John Fisher, Blackwell-Hall Factor, nephew and partner of Brice Fisher.

Nathaniel Fletcher, insurance broker.

Charles Harris, stationer to the East India Company. Married to Braund's niece.

Andrews Harrison, ironmaster.

John Harrison, ironmaster, his partner. Director of the East India Company, married to the Braunds' niece.

John Van Hemert, Dutch merchant.

Samuel Nicholson, commissioner of the Lieutenancy of the Militia, London. d. 1767.

Leonard Pead, brother-in-law of the Braunds.

John Perry, shipbuilder.

Charles Pole, M.P. for Liverpool 1756–61. West India merchant and insurer.

John Shipston. J. Shipston, Esq., was muster master general of the City Militia. d. 1766 (?). J. Shipston, broker 1748 (?).[1]

John Small, merchant and insurer.

Jacob Tonson, bookseller. Brother-in-law of Sir William Baker.

R. Wastfield, brewer.

The 'Durrington'.

It does not appear by whom she was built. Commander, first Captain Richard Crabb until 1750, then Captain Richard Drake. Husband, Samuel Braund. The accounts are incomplete for this ship, as Samuel Braund seems to have ceased to be its husband in 1751, and as William had no share in it, its further career cannot be traced. Its first two voyages do not appear to have been successful, as no dividends seem to have been declared, and a call of £80 was made on each sixteenth. The third voyage, however, brought in an unusually high dividend, £419. The owners' names were :

William Allix, grocer.

Richard Baker, director of the South Sea Company. Madeira merchant.

John Berisford, executor to Captain William Berisford, Company's commander. ·He may be the John Beresford [sic] who was at that time a Clerk of the Treasury.

John Blachford, alderman, banker ·and refiner.

[1] *A List of the Brokers of the City of London* . . ., 1748. (Guildhall Broadsides, 5. 44).

Samuel Braund, ships' husband.

R. Boddicott, West India merchant.

Sir John Chapman, Bart., M.P. for Taunton 1741–8. Sheriff of Herts. Merchant and director of the South Sea Company.

Henry Crabb (Boulton), M.P. for Worcester 1754–73. Paymaster to the East India Company until 1752. Director from 1753 to 1773. Several times Chairman.

Ambrose and John Crowley, ironmasters, successors of Sir Ambrose Crowley.

Aaron Franks, merchant.

Henry Fynes, jeweller.

Charles Gibson, of Gibson, Guildford and Orme, linen-drapers (?).

Sherman Godfrey, distiller.

Manning Lethieullier, Turkey merchant.

Nicholas Linwood, M.P. for Stockbridge 1761–8; for Aldburgh 1768–73. Director of the East India Company. Of Clermont and Linwood, Portugal merchants.

Captain John Pelly, ships' husband. Late Company's commander. Royal Exchange Assurance Director.

Charles Pole, M.P. for Liverpool 1756–61. West India merchant and insurer.

Captain Francis Steward, Company's commander.

Thomas Streatfield, linen-draper.

P. Waldo, merchant of Waldo and Eames. Had other shipping interests.

Henry Crabb Boulton was also acting on behalf of Captain Richard Gosfreight, ships' husband, late Company's commander. d. *c.* 1746, and Captain John Pelly was acting for Captain Jonathan Collet, ships' husband, late Company's commander. d. 1746.

The 'Suffolk'.

Built in the room of the *Prince of Orange* by Stanton and Wells. Commander, first Captain Richard Lewin until 1750, then Captain William Wilson. Husband, Samuel Braund. The accounts for this ship are incomplete for the same reason as for the last. Three voyages alone are covered, on which the dividends were satisfactory without being very high. The owners were:

1. *Sent in by Captain William Wilson.*

Sir Stephen Anderson, Bart.

Miles Barne. Miles Barne, Junior, M.P. for Dunwich 1741–54 and 1764–80. Miles Barne, Senior, had been in 1738 chief of one of the two Councils of Supercargoes of the East India Company at Canton,[1] and in 1733 and 1736–9 a director of the Company, but the last year he became insane,[2] and died in 1743.

Joseph Bird, sail-maker.

Captain Robert Bootle, director of the East India Company. Late Company's commander.

Nathaniel Elwick, late Governor of Madras 1714–21. Had considerable shipping interests.

Charles Pole, M.P. for Liverpool 1756–61. West India merchant and insurer.

John Sheron, cooper.

Miles Smith.

Captain William Wilson, for M. Smith.

2. *Received by Samuel Braund.*

Samuel Braund, ships' husband.

Ynyr Burges, Clerk in the office of the Company's secretary. After 1752 assistant warehouse keeper.

J. Cookson, linen-draper.

Nicholas and Thomas Crisp, insurance brokers.

Ambrose and John Crowley, ironmasters, successors of Sir Ambrose Crowley.

Thomas Grainger, closely connected with Captain John Thomlinson, see above.

Charles Harris, stationer to the East India Company. Married to the Braunds' niece.

John Harrison, ironmaster. Director of the East India Company. Married to the Braunds' niece.

John Shakespear, rope-maker.

Captain Samuel Wilson, Company's commander. Had considerable shipping interests.

Stanton and Wells, shipbuilders.

The ' Warren'.

Built by Stanton and Wells. Commander, Captain Alphonsus Glover. Husband, Samuel Braund. Here, too, the accounts are incomplete. She began with the disastrous voyage described by her commander in his letter already quoted. The result was great expense in refitting, and heavy damage to cargo, and a dispute between the Commander and the Company authorities in India. The Company ' allowed them for their losses and Expenses occasioned by a Storm the said Ship met with on the Coast of Mallabar Outward bound '[3],

---

[1] H. B. Morse, *The East India Company Trading to China, loc. cit.*
[2] Ct. Bk. 59, f. 163.   [3] Ct. Bk. 65, f. 308.

allowed the owners £1,600, but even then a call of £270 a sixteenth had to be made. The second voyage, the only other included in these accounts, was also poor, bringing in a dividend of only £180 a sixteenth. The owners were:

John Beauvois, of Pullen and Beauvois, rope-makers.

Sold to

Captain Benjamin Fisher, Company's commander.
Richard Benyon, director of the East India Company. Late Governor of Madras.
Joseph Bird, sail-maker.
Samuel Braund, ships' husband.
Thomas Burfoot, packer.
Ambrose and John Crowley, ironmasters, successors of Sir Ambrose Crowley.
John Filks.
Captain Alphonsus Glover, Company's commander.
Sir Edward Ironside, Lord Mayor of London in 1753. Of Ironside and Belchier, bankers.
Captain John Misenor, Company's commander and supercargo.
Sir Samuel Pennant, Lord Mayor of London in 1750. West India merchant.

Sold to

Moses and Raphael Franco, merchants and financiers.
Francis Salvador, merchant and financier.
John Sheron, cooper.
Captain John Smith, Company's commander.
Stephen Smith.
W. Warden, merchant.
Abraham Wells, shipbuilder.

The ' Shaftesbury '.

Built by John Perry & Co. Commander, Captain Matthew Bookey. This, the last of the ships in which Samuel Braund was concerned, has hardly the right to a place, for his connexion with it only lasted for five months, in the earlier stages of its building. It was then taken over by Captain Charles Raymond. One can, however, obtain a list of its owners, all of whom appear to have been brought together by the commander, Captain Bookey, and who seem quite outside Braund's usual connexions.

E. Bookey, wine merchant.
Ann Bookey, Senior } relatives of the commander.
Ann Bookey, Junior

John Brooke, stationer. Sheriff of London.
Pierce Galliard, of Elming near Southampton. Formerly of Lincoln's
  Inn.
Sir Samuel Gower, Kt., sail-cloth maker. Justice of Middlesex.
J. Mosseley or Moseley, of London Yard Road.
Edward Payne of J. E. & R. Payne, East India merchants. J. Payne
  was a director of the East India Company.
John Sheron, cooper.
Sir Josiah Styles, Bart., of Wateringbury, Kent. d. 1769.

INDEX OF PROPER NAMES